THE MADIBA APPRECIATION CLUB

THE MADIBA APPRECIATION CLUB

A Chef's Story

BRETT LADDS

JONATHAN BALL PUBLISHERS
JOHANNESBURG & CAPE TOWN

*I am honoured to dedicate this book to my all –
my life, my wife, Tracey Ladds.
Thanks to you, I am whole.*

All rights reserved.
No part of this publication may be reproduced or transmitted,
in any form or by any means, without prior permission
from the publisher or copyright holder.

© Text Brett Ladds 2018
© Photos Brett Ladds; p 65 © Jacoline Prinsloo
© Published edition 2018 Jonathan Ball Publishers

Published in South Africa in 2018 by
JONATHAN BALL PUBLISHERS
A division of Media24 (Pty) Ltd
PO Box 33977
Jeppestown
2043

ISBN 978-1-86842-866-3
ebook ISBN 978-1-86842-867-0

Every effort has been made to trace the copyright holders and to obtain their permission for the use of copyright material. The publishers apologise for any errors or omissions and would be grateful to be notified of any corrections that should be incorporated in future editions of this book.

Twitter: www.twitter.com/JonathanBallPub
Facebook: www.facebook.com/JonathanBallPublishers
Blog: http://jonathanball.bookslive.co.za/

Cover by Simon Richardson
Editing by Angela Voges
Design and typesetting by Martine Barker
Set in Adobe Caslon Pro/Gill Sans

Printed by **novus print**, a Novus Holdings company

Contents

Author's note viii

1 An English boytjie between a rock and a hard place 1
2 Becoming a chef 14
3 I was there 33
4 Meeting the president properly 38
5 Moving in with Madiba 50
6 'Life seems to work things out for us' 67
7 A rough ride 92
8 Receiving royalty 106
9 From Russia to the Vatican – with love 137
10 The president's birthday 164
11 Africa comes south 169
12 Rolls-Royces, cash and snipers 190
13 Moonwalking with the stars 203
14 Life after Tata 215
15 Taking flight 229

A selection of recipes by Christian Michel 241
Acknowledgements 247

Author's note

IT HAS TAKEN ME A LONG TIME to finally sit down and write this book. I think it has a lot to do with me not being very scholarly; that's why I became a chef.

You might find that I have a rather different way of putting things, but please allow me to be me. This is the only way you, the reader, will see things through my eyes.

This book is not about politics. It is about the people I've met, the food I've prepared and the experiences I've had over the past two or three decades. Even though I cooked for many politicians, I never got involved in politics. In fact, I specifically kept away from it.

1
An English boytjie between a rock and a hard place

I was born in Middelburg – a real one-horse town. My dad was a mine manager, so we moved around a lot to different mines. I have lived in every shitty part of the country you can think of.

Life at home was just as crap. On a typical weekend morning, all of us kids would lie in bed with fear washing over us like waves beating the shoreline. The house was so quiet I could hear my siblings' lips quivering at the thought of the day to come. We'd be alert to any noise from the main bedroom, where the beast had his chamber. It was a rule: we were to be awake before his dark shadow engulfed the passage.

Through fear, we learnt how to survive: we studied the beast's routine, which gave us a chance to escape the wrath that he might cast upon us. When we'd hear a sound, the starting gun would explode in our heads. We would all jump out of bed. First survival tactic: ensure that our beds were made with military precision. We'd even get down on our knees to brush the pile of the carpet into one direction. We grew up privileged, so we had our own bathroom. This allowed us to freshen up for the day even faster.

The chamber's door would start to open. Every squeak of the hinges would sound like a thousand slaves crying out for mercy. It would chill our bones. We'd know what was coming. Like a sudden breeze whispering through a window, we'd swish to our bedroom doors and paint the happiest, most loving smiles onto our faces to greet our master and wish him the most beautiful day.

His first child would survive by attempting a smile as the beast popped his head into his bedroom to ensure that everything was up to standard. He'd walk past my sister, giving her a royal nod and slowly pushing her door open. Time would slow down as I'd see her books scattered all over the floor. As his piercing eyes would start to analyse the room, I would see the plutonium reaching boiling point. All the signs would be there that this nuke was going to explode.

'Daddy, sorry about the books. I've been studying all night,' my sister would say.

The plutonium would cool. 'That's great to see,' His Lordship would say.

I would stand there and think to myself, *You little bullshitter. How the hell am I going to cap that?*

It would be my turn next. I would glance around to ensure I'd missed *nothing*.

As my head would swivel like an owl on alert, I'd see something 'scary' like a drop forming on my basin tap. I would brush my teeth over the bath while polishing the basin so it would shine; I knew this would ruin the whole day for all of us.

Using the telekinesis I believed I had, which was just as bad as my school marks, I would try to push the drop back up the tap. Trying so hard that I would not realise that He'd be standing before me.

'Are you fine?'

'Yes, Dad. Why?'

'You look constipated.'

'Sorry, Dad. I'm fine, I promise. I really promise, Dad. I'm fine.'

He'd start to walk down the passage, glancing back at me, confused. Relief would fall from me like leaves from a tree on a windy autumn morning.

The three of us would look at each other. Phase 1: we'd survived.

As if staying in crappy places was not enough, I was English-speaking, my dad was the mine manager and my sister was hot (not that I thought so – please!). Now, you may wonder what this has to do with anything. Well, here it is.

You see, the majority (wait, let me not lie – 99.8 per cent) of the population at every mine we lived on was Afrikaans-speaking. When I was growing up, it was still the days of the National Party. For all the Afrikaans kids, another kid's being English was code for *moer daai soutpiel*. When I got onto the bus in the mornings to go to school, I felt like a chicken playing among the wolves in the forest. Sitting on the cold seat, I would face forwards and avoid flinching, regardless of what projectile was thrown at me. I was too scared even to shiver from the cold in case someone took that as a challenge to fight.

The highlight of the day came when I got off the bus in the afternoons. I would always be met with a posse of '*manne vannie myn* (men from the mine)'. They would pick a boy from their group to fight me. According to their maths, an even fight meant it had to be a boy double my size and a few years older than me (a brain cell among them would be a golden prize). They justified this by his being a year or two behind me in school, as if it was my fault that he was a dumbass.

The beating would commence, with fists landing all over me. I would close my eyes to avoid getting another black eye and just windmill my arms, trying to get a punch in – or at least to block one. They thought they were clever, but I outsmarted them in the sense that this gave my sister, who was two years older than me, the chance to slip off and run home. When I saw that she had an ample head start, I would fall to the ground and check where my school case was before jumping up and, in a split second, grabbing my bag and bolting home.

My challenger would always chase me for a while with his posse cheering him on. Then he would give up with a loud shout to remind me this was not the last time I'd feel his fists – as if I'd not worked it out by then. It was the same story at every mine we moved to, just different idiots.

Despite these circumstances, I did start making friends elsewhere on the mine. It was usually a brisk walk through the veld to the mine 'compound' where the black workers lived. I was always welcomed there by the adults and the children, as my dad was a fair manager who did much to help improve the living conditions of the black workforce. My father thought the migrant labour system, where men stayed in hostels and could only see their families on their annual leave, was inhumane. At every mine we moved to, my father had housing built for families.

He also did away with a policy whereby black miners had to wear a metal armband containing their details and which section they worked in, since he felt it was humiliating. I also know that he was one of the first mine managers to start promoting black miners and placing black men in charge of white men, which was unheard of during that era. The reason I knew this was that, when he started changing all these policies, a brick was thrown at our house now and again and we got security around our home.

If only he'd been the same man at home that he was at work, doing humane things and being the upstanding man whom others saw him to be. Obviously, he'd leave that jacket at the door when he came home.

But, because of all the good work that my dad did for the mine, I was accepted by my black friends and could play with them until the sun set. My parents had no problem with this. When we would move and I would make new friends, the black families would always struggle to understand how this white boy knew all the games and enjoyed eating pap and runaways (chicken heads and feet) out of the pot.

This is one thing I have to thank my father for.

Why didn't my parents do anything about the bullying, you might wonder? The following incident may explain things.

One afternoon, when I got off the bus and the same ritual started, the boys chose a guy called Duncan to fight me. I will never forget his name. After the beating, as I dropped to look for my school case, this fat jelly pig decided he was going to pin my ass to the ground and fall on top of me. I say 'fall' and not 'jump' because there was no way gravity would let that lardass off the ground in the first place.

I felt like I was drowning with him on top of me. I could not breathe, so I decided to try to bite my way out of the situation. As soon as I started, he rolled off, yelping like a sea lion that had been kicked in the nuts. I grabbed my bag and ran home, as I always did.

The next afternoon I got off the bus and, to my surprise, all the kids moved away from me as I walked past. I was as confused as hell, to say the least. I walked slowly, expecting a trick to be played on me, yet nothing happened. As soon as I felt safe enough, I started running home. When I got there, I pumped my fist in the air with an overwhelming sense of victory. What a great day.

The next moment I saw Dad's car in the driveway with our driver Shorty standing next to it, looking at me as if I were his last-born being shipped off to war. I greeted him, but he just looked at me and said, 'Sorry, little boy.'

I was so full of joy and happiness that I had not been beaten that it took me a while to remember what it usually meant when my dad was home during work hours. The only time he would not be on the mine during the day was to inform a family that they had lost a member to an accident in or on the mine.

As I walked into the house, I saw my dad, my mom, Duncan's mom and Duncan sitting at the kitchen table. My father proceeded to question me about the events of the previous day. I told my father everything that had happened. He told me to apologise to Duncan and his mom for what I'd done and to leave the rest to him.

They had barely walked out the front door when my father slapped me across my face. It felt like I had been hit by an eighteen-wheel truck. Then, his belt tanned my body with every well-placed stroke.

After the hiding, he demanded that I wipe my tears and man up. He proceeded to inform me that I had humiliated him. As always, he reminded me that he was the boss of the mine and that he did not expect this kind of behaviour from me. I tried to explain the situation to him but then I saw him raise his hand, so I thought it best to keep quiet.

To this day, I believe he knew what was happening but chose not to get involved. So, not only did I get my afternoon beating that day, but in future I also stopped swinging my fists when I was bullied in case I landed a punch and my dad got to hear about it.

Despite all the experiences I faced on a daily basis, whether at home or on the mine, I always had one thing to look forward to: the Saturday night supper session. Given the position my dad held in the mining company, we were constantly attending functions and going out for dinner in the best restaurants that South Africa had to offer. This is where he would show off his picture-perfect family, fake smiles and gentle hugs and all. We would sit through the meals, from seven-course meals to buffets, being seen and not heard. I would always take time to study my food: we would have to eat at his pace, and he believed that chewing food for longer helped the digestion. Obviously, we all had to follow suit.

I would taste each item on my plate with my eyes closed and try to identify what it was. Then, I would start mixing the items on my plate to taste how they would change. I would always ask for all the condiments and side orders of sauces. This would allow me to play my game of stretching out each course.

Now, on Saturday nights, my dad – a would-be foodie – would

try to recreate a dish we'd eaten that week. I'd have all the time in the world to eat each dish, so I built up the courage to participate. When he realised that I added value to his experience, cooking became our thing. My sister had her great marks, my brother was the apple of my dad's eye, and now – now, we had this. On Saturday nights, for a few hours of my week, he would *see* me; I'd get no beatings and we'd actually speak. Needless to say, I started studying my dishes more and more, and tried different dishes every time we went out to eat.

I was working on our thing.

Yet the next day would always dawn, and my grey, gloomy week would commence.

Moving from school to school every time my dad was promoted had a major effect on my primary school education, as all the schools had different syllabuses or would be on different parts of the syllabus. I struggled to keep up, and it showed in my marks.

When it was time for high school, I followed in the Ladds tradition by going to Pretoria Boys High School. When I went for the interview with the headmaster, 'The Boss' Schroder, he asked me which boarding house I preferred. I jumped up with pride.

'Rissik House, sir! The one my dad and uncle went to.'

Despite his knowing that my self-esteem was at an all-time low from my great days on the mine, my father turned around and told the headmaster that I would not be staying in Rissik House since I did not deserve the honour of staying in the same house as him.

The headmaster stood up, walked around his desk, propped me up in my chair and looked into my eyes. At that moment, I felt he could see into my soul. With kindness, he told me that he would be honoured to have me in his school and that there was a special spot for me in Solomon House.

My head was spinning. I felt elated, despite my dad's hostility … all because someone had acknowledged me.

I was so proud to be going to this school with such a great

headmaster, a man who had stood up to my dad. It was the happiest day of my life until then.

It will therefore not come as a surprise that my years at Pretoria Boys High were amazing. I was never the brightest or the fastest, but I participated in everything I could and tried my best. I made wonderful friends and the worst days at boarding school were still far better than the best days at home on the mine.

I would build my confidence at school only to have it ripped out when I went home. But, as I had outsmarted the bullies, so I outsmarted my dad. All I had to do was break a few hostel rules, which got me six lashings on the ass and the 'punishment' of being gated for the weekend. I wouldn't have to go home: a win-win situation for me.

I eventually got my matric. On the last day of school, my mother came to fetch me and took me to Café Florian in Brooklyn Mall for lunch. I told her how I was looking into studying Law at the University of Pretoria – or, even better, taking a gap year to go overseas. I was baffled when my mother didn't seem to share my excitement.

Finally, she broke the news to me that my dad was not prepared to fund my tertiary education. She told me that I was on my own now, and that he felt he had done all he could for me. In great confusion, I asked why my sister had been allowed to repeat her first year at university and why he was still paying for her. My mom looked at me with sad eyes.

After an uncomfortable silence, she asked what I planned to do. I looked around me and said the first thing that came into my mind.

'In three months' time, I'll be the manager of Café Florian,' I said confidently. 'I will make a success of my life and show Dad I am worth the effort.'

Funny how we are always trying to please those who don't have time for us.

I went home to Witbank that day and packed as much as I could into a kitbag. Within days, I was off to Pretoria again. As I walked out, I turned to look at my dad.

'You will always be a fuck-up,' were his parting words.

In Pretoria, I moved in with a friend who lived in Sunnyside and got a job as a waiter at Café Florian. I was determined; after all, I had a point to prove.

It was 1992, two years after Nelson Mandela had been released and the liberation movements unbanned. However, even as the CODESA (Convention for a Democratic South Africa) talks for a democratic government continued, the country was in turmoil, with much political unrest and violence. At work, there was even tension between the black kitchen staff and the white employees.

Every morning, I would catch a taxi from Sunnyside to Brooklyn. You could spot this white boy from a mile away in the taxi (in those days, it was unheard of for white people to take a 'black' taxi). As luck would have it, one of the black chefs took the same taxi. We got chatting and from that point we got on very well.

In the mornings, before or after my shift, I would often go to the kitchen to talk and joke around with the kitchen staff. I assisted with the prepping of the food and eventually also helped to cook food.

One day, the staff could not come to work due to political unrest. The kitchen was empty and the owner was in a panic. I offered to help. I remember starting to take out the prep for the day. The next moment, I was cooking. Before I knew it, it was closing time. It dawned on me that I had loved every moment. The following day, I spoke to the owner and asked if I could rather work in the kitchen as a kitchen hand. In those days, very few restaurants had chefs; most of the kitchen staff had no formal training. She was elated.

As time went by, the atmosphere in the kitchen improved. There was laughter and a happy, joyful vibe. From the first day, I knew this was what I wanted to do – in the kitchen was where I belonged.

A while later, centre management approached the owner of Café Florian. They needed someone to cater for clients who put up displays or presented shows at the centre. The owner thought I would be perfect for it, so I also started catering for functions in the mall.

Word spread fast about the tasty food I was making. At the time, Café Florian was the place to be seen, and people noticed the improved quality of the meals on offer. When we did the catering for functions, everyone spoke about the food. While I had no training, I had quite some flair. I would combine foods to create unique yet mind-exploding tastes, having had all that time to experiment during the long lunches and dinners my family had had to attend. I'd use fortified wines in my chicken roulades, and made combinations such as liquorice and sesame seed salmon, habanero, chocolate and beef spear fondues, and gammon lollipops served in gluhwein.

Then, the day came that would change my life forever. I was in the kitchen when a waitress walked in and said there were clients who wanted to see me. Now, you need to know one thing about the restaurant business: when there is praise to be had, the owner is usually the first one to run and lap it up. When the owner isn't around, the waitress normally takes the credit by telling the client she had made a special request. So, the chefs rarely get direct praise; I walked out with trepidation, expecting a complaint.

There before me sat the most distinguished, larney couple. Their expensive perfume and cologne lingered in the air. Their diamonds and gold glittered like the sun shimmering on the Mediterranean. Everything about them said Waterkloof.

'Great day to you, madam, sir. How may I be of assistance?' I asked.

'This was one of the best breakfasts I have ever had,' the gentleman said in a French accent. His elegant wife tilted her head and gave me the most beautiful smile.

I thanked them, even though I was still waiting for the catch. Then the refined gentleman asked me if I had used Scottish salmon.

'Sir, I only use the best,' I said. *Well, the best the owner would pay for*, I thought to myself. He then asked again if it was Scottish salmon. I leant forward, so that other tables couldn't hear, and told him that I was not, in fact, sure what kind of salmon it was, but that the rep who sold it always told me it was the best. They thanked me, and I was on my way.

A few days later they were back. Again, I was summoned to the front. As I peered out of the hatch, I recognised them. This time, I was confident and positive when I went out to speak to them.

When Christian Michel introduced himself and his wife, Judy, in his thick accent, even their names sounded fancy. His hand was big, with the strength of a vice grip, yet the skin was rough and hard. In light of his appearance, I had expected strong, but soft, hands.

It turned out that they were regular customers and had noticed the difference in the food since I had started working in the kitchen.

I was quite surprised when they asked me whether I had ever been trained in the industry. I proceeded to tell them the story of how I became a waiter and how I landed up working in the kitchen. Christian then asked me to sit down as he wanted to speak to me. He was so charismatic and encouraging that I grabbed the closest chair.

While he didn't divulge much about himself, he mentioned that he was a chef. He asked me a few general questions before he took the wind out of my sails: 'Would you like formal training as a chef?'

Not taking anything for granted, I told him I had to work to pay the bills and could not take time off for training.

'What if I made an arrangement that would allow you to be trained by me?' Christian asked.

Ja, sure, I thought sceptically. Then he took out a pen and wrote down their address and asked if I could come to see them after my shift the next day. I swear, even his handwriting was immaculate.

I could have framed that piece of paper! And I was right – they lived in Waterkloof.

I was intrigued, though unsure about where all this was leading. The following day, after my shift, I walked from Brooklyn to Waterkloof, a forty-minute walk. The Michels lived in an impressive white house with massive gates. And there I was with sweat on my brow, my hair in a mess and my backpack stuck to my back in the scorching heat. I took out some deodorant, did a quick spray, tried to finger-comb my hair, and rubbed the tops of my shoes on my calves to give them a shine. I decided not to take my backpack off – nothing I could do would suddenly evaporate the sweat off my back, which felt like swampland.

I rang the bell and was greeted by little barking Yorkies. Christian opened the door with a warm smile, picked up the dogs and welcomed me in. The house was filled with expensive furniture and the carpets looked like rolling fields of golden threads.

As we walked to the kitchen, I saw a number of photos on display. There was Christian standing next to different presidents, and not just one or two. I realised then that this man had to be someone of stature.

When we got to the kitchen, I was amazed by its size. Café Florian's kitchen would've fitted in his pantry. There was a cold room and enough equipment on shelves to open up a supply chain. Needless to say, it was done with taste and tact; everything belonged right where it was.

I asked Christian about the photos and how he had managed to meet all those famous people. That was the moment I learnt that he was the government's executive chef and managed the Diplomatic Guesthouse, where all the government's guests were hosted. For decades, he had been both the chef and the manager of the Diplomatic Guesthouse.

After telling me more about his work, there was a sudden pause.

Christian looked me straight in the eye. 'You know, Brett, I never had a son ...'

Christian leant forward, held my shoulders with his disturbingly large hands and said, 'To be born stupid is acceptable, but to die stupid is sad. I want to pass all my knowledge on to you, to avoid dying stupid!'

I was speechless. Here, this virtual stranger wanted to give me what money could not buy – his knowledge and experience. I asked whether I would be trained at the Diplomatic Guesthouse.

'No,' he answered, 'I have been retired for over a year now. I will train you here at my house.'

In walked Judy, looking incredible. 'Do you realise that we've met before?' she asked with a broad smile. She passed me a photograph of her holding a child. 'This is you, at your christening.'

Judy explained that she knew my grandparents and also my mom from when she was a child. She and my grandparents had been neighbours and, when my mom and her siblings were still at school, they used to climb over the fence and swim in Judy's pool. They were close friends, which is why Judy was at my christening. However, after my parents had started moving around to different mines, she and my mom had lost contact.

Christian again asked if I would be interested. I could not say yes quickly enough.

2
Becoming a chef

And so began my apprenticeship under Chef Christian Michel. All the while, I was working at Café Florian. The owners were elated that I would be getting proper training and gave me the necessary time off.

Master Christian was adamant that I had to learn the trade in the traditional, old-fashioned way: for the first two years, I was not allowed to use any modern kitchen equipment. He said it was only after I had been trained that I would be ready to start making use of modern technology.

That might sound reasonable, and charming in an old-school kind of way. But *you* try making steak tartare this way: the recipe calls for, among others, a kilogram of *freshly ground* beef striploin. So, I walked over to Christian and asked for the mincer. He smiled and handed me a knife. I sniggered, assuming he was deaf or preoccupied, and asked for the mincer again. He turned and looked at me as if I had just forgotten the veal roast in the oven, leaving it to burn.

'No, no, no, no,' he said and slapped me on the back with a hand as hard as a rock. 'Ze knife, use ze knife!'

I took the knife and started cutting, then chopping, the huge piece of fillet he had given me. I can do this, I told myself. It took me at least forty minutes, but once I was done the meat was fine. I had also been washing the board the whole time to avoid cutting the blood into the meat. I then shaped it and walked over to Chef Christian.

My hands were raw. Even my calluses were blistered. I stood there, proud as a puppy that had caught his first bird.

Chef put his hand on my back, looked me in the eye and said disapprovingly, 'My boy, my dad always said – if you have not ears, better have good hands.'

What could be wrong? He had handed me the meat, so it was the right meat. He had given me the knife, so it was the right knife. He had watched me chop the meat, so I must've done it correctly. I asked him to explain.

He then took his big, sausage-like fingers and dug into my masterpiece. He scratched out some tiny – as in miniature – white pieces.

'Look, sinew in ze meat. No, no, no!'

My head sagged and my shoulders dropped in disbelief. Chef fetched another piece of meat and told me to try again. Of the numerous life and chef lessons Chef Christian taught me, the most important was probably to do everything correctly – it had to be perfect – or not do it at all.

During the two years that I trained under Chef Christian Michel, I was taught, and experienced, traditional French culinary skills. He held back on nothing – the produce, meats and fish I trained with were always world-class. I was also blessed to have drunk wines, champagnes and other alcoholic beverages of the finest quality from around the world.

At the beginning of 1994, I was allowed to cook by myself in my training. By then, I was two months away from my twenty-first birthday in March. Chef said he felt I was ready; by then, I was dying to show off my expertise and craftsmanship. I wanted to stop cheffing at Café Florian and move to a bigger platform to showcase my craftsmanship.

One evening, I was at the Michels' house after my shift. I often made them dinner. That night, crayfish was on the menu. They were drinking Dom Perignon, their favourite. While we were busy with our meal, the phone rang.

Even though I had eaten there hundreds of times, I had never noticed the phone. As I turned around, I started to snigger. The phone Christian answered was actually red – like the ones you would see in the movies. Judy leant forward and asked me what was so funny.

'This phone looks like a hotline to the president,' I said. She told me to pipe down and listen.

Then I heard Christian say, 'Pik, no, I am retired. I have left the department. I am not interested.'

In a whisper, I asked Judy if it could really be the Minister of Foreign Affairs, Pik Botha, on the line. From the photos in their house, I knew this was a strong possibility. Judy smiled and nodded. 'The one and only.'

After a brief conversation, Chef Christian sat down without saying a word. He simply carried on pulling the white meat out of his crayfish shell and dipping it into his sauce béarnaise. Judy turned to him gracefully and asked about the call.

He informed us that Pik had asked whether he would help out for a few months. The National Party government believed the ANC was going to win the elections and the Department of Foreign Affairs wanted to prepare what would become known as the Presidential Guesthouse for the inauguration of the new president and to cater for dignitaries visiting Nelson Mandela and the ANC.

'Was that really Pik Botha? Will you be cheffing for the new president? Are you sure you heard right?'

I was so curious I could die. '*Assez* (Enough),' Christian said with great authority. It took a few minutes for the news to sink in and for him to realise what a great opportunity this could be – the grand finale of his career.

I sipped my champagne. The silence lasted for a minute or two before I asked Chef whether he would consider it. He looked at Judy, who said she felt they should be part of history in the making and that it would be an honour.

Judy then turned to me and told me not to utter a word of what had just happened to anyone. They would let me know if Christian decided to accept the job. Our glasses shot to the middle of the table, crystal on crystal ringing out followed by Christian saying, '*À ta santé!* (cheers!)'

After dinner, I was so excited by the possibility of doing something great with my training that I ran all the way from Waterkloof to Café Florian. It felt like I had floated there. Even though I had to keep mum, at least I could be excited among friends. When I got there, I walked around with a smile that even acid could not burn off my face.

That night I simply couldn't fall asleep. I washed all my chef's jackets and pants, then ironed them three times. I kept looking at my phone (then still a landline) in the hope that Chef would call to say he was taking the job … and taking me with him.

When I started my shift in the kitchen the next morning, I kept looking through the hatch to see if Chef would drop by. But he was nowhere to be seen and my heart started to sink. Later that afternoon, the owner called me to say I had a call. Walking to the phone, I assumed it was a supplier about an order. I answered with a disheartened voice. But it was Chef! He asked if I would join him the next day to go to the Presidential Guesthouse to see what was expected. He told me to be at his house at 9 a.m. I was so busy agreeing with him that I was not quite listening.

'Shhhh now!' he said. 'If this is what you want to do, you have to do the honourable thing and inform the owners that you will be leaving Café Florian.'

'Yes, Chef! I will, Chef.'

At first, leaving Café Florian was just a speed bump. Then it started to feel like I was about to break up with the girlfriend I'd loved for a long time. The owners had been so good to me. I knew I'd repaid them through my time, service and loyalty, but I still felt that I owed them. I really did not know how to tell them. They had other businesses, so I knew that they took calls at all hours. I phoned them and explained the situation. They were saddened. Worse, they understood and were their typical awesome selves about it. They even told me that if things did not work out, there would always be a space for me at Café Florian.

As I stood cooking for the rest of my shift, I realised something: this was growth. I was not dying, just moving on. To be honest, tears were spilt. I mourned for my first team and my first love, my small kitchen.

It took a few hugs and kisses from the waitresses to help me see the bigger picture. I baked a huge cake for the owner and my team.

I was done by 10 p.m. and ran back home to Sunnyside. I bathed, got dressed and sat on my bed, watching the seconds tick by.

Finally, the sun came up. I took my jacket off and folded it neatly before placing it in a plastic bag. I shone my shoes – again – and placed them in another plastic bag. I put the two plastic bags into my backpack before changing into a T-shirt and takkies. It was 7 a.m.

I decided to walk slowly: I would sweat less and keep my crisp look. Still, I got there just before 8 a.m. – I was so excited that my left foot tried to beat my right foot. I stood outside Christian's house for a while to cool down – the excitement combined with the brisk walk had made me a bit hot. At about 08:40 I put my chef's jacket and shoes on, fixed my hair and drowned myself in deodorant.

At 9 a.m. sharp, the massive white gates opened. I walked into the house, and Christian and I had coffee and a roll. I could barely contain my excitement. Then, the moment finally came. It was time to go. I must've looked like a kid about to go to the circus, because every time Chef looked at me, he laughed. He had a Rolls-Royce and three Jaguars. I waited to see which car he would pick. He finally opened the door of the XJS V12. It was pearl white and fast as hell. Getting in, I knew we looked the part.

As we drove down Church Street, I could see Bryntirion Estate. Right in the middle of the estate was the Presidential Guesthouse. As we got closer to the gate, all you could see were blue lights. My heartbeat quickened and my mouth went dry. I heard the car gear down. Next thing, Christian turned on the indicator.

As we drove down a long, dead-straight road, we saw security everywhere. The police wore bulletproof vests and carried automatic rifles. Some had dogs, others metal detectors. I was trying desperately to take it all in. Frankly, I was in awe. It was as if I had stepped into an action movie.

At a circle, we turned left then immediately right into a walled-off quad. This was the back of the guesthouse's kitchen. There were a few black gentlemen standing at high-end cars that were so clean they blinded you. The men were well-dressed and well-built, and their shoes were shimmering – they looked like warriors from King Shaka's training camp.

The moment we got out of the car, these suited warriors started interrogating us. 'Why are you here? What do you want? Go, you are not wanted here.'

I started retreating to the car, all the joy I'd felt and the dreams I'd had on the way to the guesthouse evaporating. The next moment, my thoughts turned to fear. In a split second, the verbal attack had put me into survival mode. The guys were towering over us and moving forward. At that point, Christian shouted, 'Enough!'

We all froze. Even the pride of lions ready to rip us apart took a step back.

'We have been invited here!' he said.

'Do you know who we are?' asked the leader of the group.

'No,' said Christian. 'We have not had the honour of being introduced.'

Now the leader sported a huge frown on his face. The rest of the group gave us killer stares. In a trembling voice, and with all the respect I could muster I said, 'Sorry to speak, sirs, but this is Mr Michel. He is the former Executive Chef of South Africa and he is very French. He is trying to tell you that we were asked here by the government to come and cook at the guesthouse.'

As I spoke, all 106 kilograms of me quivered like a blade of grass in a field during a storm.

'Oh, why didn't you just say so? Kitchen's that way,' Mr Leader said, pointing in the direction of the back door.

'Send us food, we are hungry,' a voice shouted after us.

WHEN WE ENTERED the building, we walked down a few passages. It was obvious that Christian knew where he was going, but to me it was a sixteenth-century maze. I felt that the walls were going to attack me, that the doors could cause bodily harm. At that stage, I could not appreciate the architecture or how well maintained the building was.

As we turned a corner, there stood Pik Botha. He greeted Christian in his deep-barrel voice, then I was introduced. Pik asked Christian if all was fine. I wanted to jump in and start explaining the experience we'd just had, but Christian briefly and calmly explained what had happened.

'It was the usual, Pik. Everyone wants to be a hero.'

What? Was this supposed to be the norm? I thought. *If so, what the hell am I doing here?*

Pik and Christian chatted for a while and reminisced about the past before he explained the situation to Christian. He needed us to assist with setting up the Presidential Guesthouse for the VVVIP guests, and help with the inauguration ceremony of our new president, Nelson Mandela.

While they were still discussing details, I asked whether I could look around. 'That won't be a problem, but avoid the Pink Room because the top echelon of the ANC is meeting in there,' Pik warned. I decided not to go into any room with a closed door as I didn't exactly know where the Pink Room was.

Entrance to the west wing of the Presidential Guesthouse.

On my walkabout, I first discovered the main kitchen. It was huge, roughly two hundred square metres, with a scullery on the side of about a hundred and twenty square metres. The equipment was old, but neatly polished. You could see every bump in it, yet it glittered. The floors were old; in their heyday, the tiles could have been light beige. The tiles on the walls were so brilliantly white I felt as heaven had descended.

The kitchen was on the second floor. I walked down and saw the glass scullery, which was just as crisp and clean, even if it showed wear and tear. I knew this scullery could tell many a story.

Opposite the glass scullery was a dining room. The walls were panelled with a deep, rich wood that had years of conversations polished into it with a glossy wax. As you walked in, you felt history coming at you like a champion boxer at a punching bag. The carpet had wear marks where many a politician had walked to be seated at the table in the centre. The table was ridiculously long and big – I counted sixty-four chairs. Noticing the velvety green curtains, a feeling of sadness came over me. Here was this beautiful room with all its history that was begging to be your host for the evening, but her dress was old and slightly worn.

A view from the gardens on the east side, looking towards the Presidential Guesthouse. Part of the presidential inauguration ceremony was held here.

I walked out the way I had come in, and turned right into the passage. The double door on the left was locked, but I looked through the leaded glass and saw the legs and frame of the most beautiful, solid-wood pool table, which was covered with a white cloth. It looked like a corpse in a mortuary. I then realised that this fine building had not been used in a long time, even if it had been well maintained. *Why hadn't previous presidents used it?* I wondered.

I continued down the passage and saw the Breakfast Room or Green Room (named for the colour it was painted), which contained an eight-seater table. I didn't know much about interior decorating at the time, but even I could see it was a decorator's nightmare. It looked as if a floral arrangement had exploded in the room. The chairs and the benches around the room were covered with the same green floral material as the curtains. I chuckled as I walked through the room, wondering which president's wife had had such poor taste.

The next big double door had two of those suited warriors standing outside – not the same ones who had jumped at us when we arrived, but they came from the same mould. I could only assume they were protecting the so-called Pink Room. As I walked past, I could feel their eyes burrowing into the back of my head.

The next room had three entrances, but only the middle double door was unlocked. It was a triple-volume room with enormous chairs that seemed to have come from the set of *Alice in Wonderland*, and looonnnggg couches. Grand chandeliers hung from the ceiling. Placed around the sides were heavy wooden cupboards, into which you could fit a small family.

I then made my way down the stairs to the front door. The stairs were the most beautiful marble, and long white pillars stood guard as I walked down the three flights. Just before I got to the landing at the bottom, three police officers shot out of a small room. They chased me back up the stairs, shouting that I did not have the right to be in that part of the house.

I continued my venture down the marble passageway, at the end of which I found an office. It had two huge wooden desks, which looked as if they had arrived in 1652 on the *Goede Hoop*. They were in mint condition and, on closer inspection, I saw they had hand-engraved brass plaques – past presidents must have used these desks. The bookshelves were filled with Afrikaans books about law and history.

Leaving the office, I took the lift to the top floor, where I discovered the bedrooms. As I walked along the passage and looked into each suite, I saw they were fit for kings and queens.

President Mandela's favourite room. The wingback chair to the left of the fireplace is where he always sat.

I took the back stairs down and ended up back in the kitchen, where I found Christian. We then made notes of what we required in terms of stock and equipment. We dropped off our list at the Department of Foreign Affairs and drove home in silence. When we stopped at Christian's house, he smiled and said, 'See you in the morning. We leave at five.'

On my walk home, I had over an hour to think about the events of the day. I was filled with mixed feelings. While I was bowled over by what I had seen in the house, I was also concerned about the harsh treatment we had received by the guards. It made me concerned, and a little scared. I had only just left Café Florian, but I was already missing it.

This was not what I thought I had signed up for.

THE FOLLOWING MORNING we reported for duty, but the staff at the guesthouse met us with extreme hostility – especially the security staff. Months later, I would learn that they saw Christian and me as yet two more white bosses … not exactly what they had envisaged in a democratic South Africa.

We found everything we had ordered the previous day from Foreign Affairs in the storerooms and fridges. However, when we started switching on the stoves and ovens, we had bodyguards and security around us all the time. They were constantly keeping tabs on us and checking what we were busy with, and not in a nice way. They questioned everything we did; even when we went to fetch something, the packet was ripped open or hit out of our hands.

When we asked to speak to someone from Protocol who could advise us how many people we had to cook for and for what time, we always got the same response: 'Just cook, that's what you are here for.' (Protocol was the department in the president's office that ran all the logistics concerning the president and his guests, including catering requirements. The Protocol staff are the government's events coordinators, so to speak.) It was terrible the number of meals we cooked that went uneaten because we had over-catered.

What made the situation even more challenging was that, not only were we supposed to chef in the guesthouse, we were also in charge of all logistics, from the suites and service to cleaning, laundry and finances. We even had our own security division.

At that stage, I was terribly upset by the animosity from the staff. I felt I had not been part of the past and hadn't had a hand in apartheid policy – I hadn't even voted in a general election yet. I continuously tried to remind myself how I would have felt if I were in their shoes and had been through what they had experienced. Yet I also hoped that the staff would notice my dedication and lack of discrimination – I was there to serve.

Sometimes we fed President Mandela, sometimes we fed the ministers, and sometimes we fed the flies. This was extremely annoying; President Mandela was staying at the guesthouse at the time, so we knew he had to eat. He was the only person staying in the east wing. The bodyguards had to be fed, too. All the president's meetings took place at the guesthouse, in the boardrooms or one of the lounges, as it was convenient for him. If there had just been more trust and transparency, it would have made our lives so much easier.

Besides, I had met the most stunning girl, Tracey. We were madly in love. I would far rather have sat and gazed at her, watching our future play out in her heavenly blue eyes, than waste my time.

At about 5 p.m. every day, the formalities would wind down and all the ANC delegates would start relaxing. Once we'd been told there'd be no top brass around for the night, Christian would head home and I would remain to serve food to the people who were still around.

The bodyguards annexed a section of the guesthouse close to Mandela's suite, where they slept and ate. There was always security. They were like cobras – you could not always see them, but you knew they were there. One wrong move and they were onto you.

I would make meals for all the bodyguards and take them upstairs to their burrow. This was the worst time of the day for me. When I entered the room, they would usually be lounging around. As I'd walk in, their heads would snake up. Sometimes I thought they were simply waiting for me to make a mistake so they could strike.

Then the comments would start. Hey whitey, this. Hey whitey, that. There were rude comments, racist jokes and biting words. To make matters worse, I would be sent up and down the stairs to fetch condiments or even just a serviette – for a few minutes, I was their entertainment. All I did was grin and bear it. Thanks to my old man and those bullies on the mines, this treatment seemed a breeze. I was always polite and kept a smile on my face, never giving anyone a reason to challenge or attack me.

Once or twice I was even kicked on the behind as I bent down to collect all the dirty crockery and cutlery, or given a nudge with an AK-47 in the ribs or the back. I did think about walking out, throwing a punch, or even reporting the abuse. But, every time, I managed to maintain my composure and walk out with a smile.

One morning, when I arrived at the guesthouse at about 4 a.m. to start prepping, I found one of the bodyguards in the kitchen in excruciating pain. He seemed cagey when I walked up to him and asked what the matter was. He told me had been shot a few years ago and suffered, consequently, from stomach pain and cramps. I went to the first aid box in the office to get Imodiums and pain tablets. I gave him a glass of water and assisted him onto a chair. I then made him an egg on toast so the tablets wouldn't burn his stomach. When he had eaten, I assisted him back upstairs to the snake burrow.

The day went as normal: we were treated like shit and given the wrong information, and food was wasted. We never knew what was going on. Throughout the day, I checked up on the bodyguard. I gave him more tablets and water every four hours, and food at mealtimes. Before I went home, I checked in on him one last time, gave him tablets again, extra for pain, and left two bottles of mineral water next to his bed.

At this point, it was a week to go before Nelson Mandela's inauguration as South Africa's first democratically elected president. There was quite a buzz around the guesthouse and security became even more stringent. The next morning, when I arrived at the locked back door, I found a group of adults and kids wrapped in blankets, trying to keep warm. I asked whether I could be of assistance, but the next moment the caretaker of the estate stormed at the group from out of the blue.

Until that point, I'd had few dealings with her, but I'd heard she was the local battle-axe. She could do what she wanted because she had family connections with the wife of a high-ranking member of the outgoing government.

'Who are these people?' she shouted.

'Sorry, Madam, I recognise the little boy and the lady standing there. They often spend time with Mr Mandela.'

Then it all came out: her true colours. 'These kaffirs won't go into the *gastehuis* (guesthouse).'

I must've looked as if I had been hit by a ten-foot pole. 'I think you are extremely rude and arrogant. They will come inside with me so I can find out why they are here,' I said.

She took the big bunch of keys, threw it at me and stormed off.

I looked around in panic. If I'd been verbally abused and kicked for feeding people, imagine what the bodyguards would do to me if I found myself in the vicinity of a fellow white who had used the k-word?

The next moment, the back door swung open and there stood a bodyguard – the one who had been ill the day before. I nearly shat myself. *Here we go,* I thought.

'Who was that? You, come with me,' he said.

I scuttled forward nervously trying to explain what had happened. I had one bodyguard in front of me and one behind me, with the kids and ladies following us. There was no response to my words; I was marched into the main lounge and told to sit down.

Sitting on another chair was Nelson Mandela, our soon-to-be president.

The bodyguard walked up and whispered something in his ear. As this was happening, the little boy ran to Mr Mandela and jumped onto his lap, and the ladies went upstairs.

I sat frozen in fear: I had passed Mr Mandela in the passage numerous times and served him when he was dining with other ANC members, but this was the first time all his attention had been focused on me.

The bodyguard walked up and grabbed me by my chef's jacket and motioned for us to go. As I walked out, I heard Mr Mandela say, 'Thank you.' I turned around to see him playing with the boy. He smiled at me and nodded.

As we walked down the passage, the bodyguard walked alongside me. All I noticed was his prominent gun. Then, he gave me a soft nudge on the shoulder.

'Hey whitey, thank you – I feel much better today.'

When we got to the kitchen, I asked, 'Am I fired? Must I go?'

'No!' he said. 'I am Victor. That miserable *madala* over there is Gigi.'

'Please to meet you, sir. I am Brett,' I replied meekly.

'Whitey, you are the chef, you cook great food. We will call you Chef.'

Gigi looked at me and gave a grumpy nod.

I couldn't hold out any longer: 'Victor, what just happened?'

'We were informed that some family members were coming but we were not dressed when they arrived. While we were getting ready, we heard what happened at the kitchen door. Trust us, that old whitey won't be seen around here again. Now, if you need anything you speak to me. I told Tata what had happened – I wanted him to see you.'

When I walked up to the bodyguards' burrow that night, I prepared myself for the usual treatment. When I put down the food, I noticed that the room was clean. I wouldn't have to tidy it up before I left. As I walked out, I even got a 'That smells nice.' I turned around and thanked the bodyguard.

A while later, I returned to fetch the dishes. This time, they were all neatly packed in a pile on the table. The bodyguards were watching soccer and cheering. I collected the plates, and said good night. 'Go well,' they shouted.

As I walked down the stairs, Victor came running after me. 'Chef, don't forget Tata will have breakfast at seven. Have it ready. It's his big day.'

That was the first time I had ever known anything about his schedule.

I went downstairs, washed the dishes and cleaned the kitchen. When I got home, I had a bath and slept like a baby. I had been seen, and appreciated.

Early one morning a few weeks later, as I was switching on the stoves and ovens, Victor popped in. I made him a cup of coffee and some toast, and asked how his stomach was.

'Much better. I haven't had any problems since last time. It must be the great food,' he said, and chuckled. We started talking about our pasts and I asked him about the shooting incident.

'It was a few years ago when I was in Angola,' he said. 'I was shot with an AK-47.'

'No way!' I said as I picked up his AK-47. 'Seriously? Where?'

Victor stood up and pulled up his shirt. On his stomach and chest were marks that looked like small, round burns. Then he turned around: zigzagging along his spine were scars that looked like his flesh had been torn from his body.

I could only imagine the pain this man had been through. I realised how committed many of the struggle activists had been when they said they would die for their cause. In front of me stood a hero to the cause who had come within an inch of his life.

'It must've been the most terrifying experience you have ever had.'

'At that time, I thought it was …'

He had me. 'Come on, Victor. Can anything be worse than being shot?'

'Well, there was one time when I was convinced I was going to be beaten to death.'

I urged him to tell me more.

'At this rate we will never eat breakfast today and Tata will have to go out for KFC – start cooking!'

I vigorously began prepping the meals in the hope that I would hear more. Victor sat down, taking a long slurp of coffee.

'Now listen, what I am about to tell you was in the news, but those bloody reporters told it in their own way. We were in a hotel in Cape Town one night after Tata was released from prison. The security guys were in the room next to Tata. We heard a noise outside and when we looked down there was a big group of Boere in bakkies. They were calling for the president. They wanted him outside.

'We grabbed our AKs and jumped into the lift, our hearts beating like a Zulu drum. When we got to the lobby we took cover. They were trying to ram the door down with a bakkie. All we could do was take aim and be ready for what happened next. We were ready for anything, back together as comrades in arms.'

Victor looked up and started laughing. 'Are you pulling my leg, Victor?' I asked.

'No, it's only now that I can see the funny side of it,' he said.

'Really, you are sick in the head, not in the stomach!'

'Shoosh man! As we were bracing ourselves for this battle, the lift opened. My first reaction was that we were being attacked from both sides. I rolled over to take aim at the lift, but who was standing in front of me? The president – tall and proud. He looked like he had all the warrior shields around him from his ancestors.

'I shouted at one of the guys who had come with him. "Why is Tata here?" Apparently, they'd had no choice. Tata was adamant that he wanted to come and speak to those people who hated him so much. By now, they had gained access to the lobby. You could feel the tension and lust for blood in the air.

'Tata walked forward and as he did so the chaos simply stopped. He asked who was in charge. Some men came forward. They looked confused and unsteady. Tata asked whether he could sit around a table with them and discuss the issues at hand.

'Initially the Boere looked at each other, not knowing what to do. Then they agreed to the meeting. Tata was adamant that no guns from either side should be in the room. We were trying to discourage the president, but our pleas fell on deaf ears. We waited outside the door. I don't think any of us budged an inch or even blinked.'

'After what felt like two sunrises, they all came out. The Boere tipped their hats and shook the president's hand respectfully. It looked like they were about to bow to him. One man even turned around and apologised. The look in his eyes seemed sincere.'

'So Tata was actually able to talk sense into their heads?'

'Yes, they went from hating hyenas to loving bunnies. I think they finally saw what we already knew about Tata for all these years.'

Victor stood up and thanked me for breakfast, and off he went to rest.

It took me a while to process this story. It sounded like something out of a movie. Over the next few weeks, I asked some of the other bodyguards about it. They all recalled the event.

3
I was there

Nelson Mandela was inaugurated as the first democratically elected president of South Africa on 10 May 1994. In the days running up to the inauguration, the guesthouse was abuzz with famous leaders and their chefs from all over the world.

Now that I had been accepted by the bodyguards, I could walk around all parts of the guesthouse and the rest of the property. A tent was erected a few metres from the guesthouse where the inauguration dinner would be held.

On the day of the inauguration, as I walked to the front entrance of the guesthouse, I had to push my way through a phalanx of bodyguards. Every celebrity, every president, every royal personality who was there had had his or her own bodyguards. However, since the guesthouse had its own security, only a few dignitaries were allowed to take their bodyguards along to the dinner – the rest had to remain outside. I must have been in the safest place in the world.

As I entered through the large wooden doors, silence descended. Only a select few dignitaries had been invited to the guesthouse to meet President Mandela; most would be escorted directly to the tent after the inauguration. Those who were on the guest list had a very strict schedule to stick to.

And here I, a mere chef, could share in the show. Walking down the long marble passage, I brushed shoulders with people who drew crowds of millions, whom people queued at the side of the road to see and TV reporters spent months trying to interview. People like

Queen Elizabeth II, Yasser Arafat, Hillary Clinton, Fidel Castro and Al Gore were sitting around as I strode by. *I am the shizzle!* I thought.

After my little tour, I headed back to the kitchen. There, I found chefs from all over the world who had been invited to chef at the inauguration. Top hospitality companies and hotel chains had been approached by the government to cater for this historic function, and many of them had brought in international chefs. Christian and I were also part of the group of invited chefs. The duties were split between the different companies, so each of us knew what was expected of us.

Of course, Christian and I watched what the other chefs were doing and stole with our eyes. As we walked past one section, I saw two Malaysian chefs, who were in charge of decoration and garnish. They took a watermelon and started making incisions in different directions. After several minutes, they turned it upside down and shook the loose pieces out – and there was a carved portrait of Madiba! I stood there with my mouth hanging open.

I asked them a few questions, but only got a smile and a nod after each question. *Was I annoying them?* I wondered. Maybe they just wanted to finish their work. Then, a British voice bellowed, 'They ain't understanding us, laddie! You're looking quite foolish. Can you stop now? My gut is aching from laughter.'

In a last-ditch effort, I gave a thumbs-up to the two gentlemen. They smiled and waved, again. I went back to my cooking station and continued with the task at hand. After a while, one of the Malaysian chefs came past with a watermelon, this time with my face on it. It was incredible to see. Being who I am, I jumped around, grabbed him and gave him a bear hug.

Well, let me tell you, that did not go down too well. I didn't understand what he was saying to his colleague but it looked like he was convinced I wanted more from him than a watermelon. In fact, I am quite sure he told me where I could put the watermelon.

For the next few hours, all the chefs worked incredibly hard. Everyone was very focused; the kitchen was so quiet you could hear a church mouse fart. Most of the guests who had been invited to the guesthouse left to prepare for the inauguration ceremony. The parking area in front of the guesthouse became much emptier. As we were going about our duties, you could feel the pride and excitement in the air.

Then, out of the blue, an elderly chef strode in as if he had slipped on a bag of carrots and one had lodged deep and tight. He was a prominent figure in the cheffing world in South Africa and worked for one of the big hotel groups. Yet the whole day, while we had been working like crazy, he'd been nowhere to be found.

In his loud, husky voice, he started shouting that we had to hurry up and that the situation was not acceptable (even though we were on schedule). He did not have one nice thing to say. Many of the South African chefs who were there had worked with him, and were clearly unsettled and alarmed by his insults. I was horrified, as he was one of the chefs I'd been looking forward to meeting.

The next moment, Christian grabbed a large pot and started beating it with a steel ladle. I thought my mentor had lost all his marbles in one throw – that his brain had finally evaporated out of his ears from all the years in front of a stove.

We all stared at Christian beating the pot in front of Mr Bullfrog Full-of-shit. Our faces were the colour of our white jackets; we stood stiffer than all the executive chefs' hats. Once Christian had silenced him, he simply turned around and went back to his station.

'Who the hell do you think you are?' Bullfrog bellowed at Christian. 'Do you know who I am?'

If it was silent before when we'd all been cooking, you could now hear crickets leopard-crawling out of the grass to get away from this one. Christian looked up and across the kitchen. 'Does anyone know who this man is? It appears he has forgotten his name.'

Everyone started sniggering while trying to maintain their composure.

'What? What did you say?' Bullfrog shouted.

Christian walked up to him with the pot and the ladle, lifted it up to eye level and said, 'Don't you find it surprising how the emptiest barrel always makes the loudest noise?'

'Let me tell you who I am!' At this point, Bullfrog could barely breathe. 'I am [name withheld] and I am in charge here, do you understand me, Frenchman?'

Christian walked back to his station, opened up his briefcase and took out a thick document. He held it up to Bullfrog. 'Have you seen this before?'

Bullfrog snatched it out of Christian's hands and looked at it. Quite proudly, Christian lowered the file and pushed it along the stainless-steel table with all the food prep.

'Yes, I have the same one right here,' Bullfrog hissed.

Christian picked up the file again and turned it around. 'Is that your name on top, where it states what is expected of you today?'

'Yes, yes it is!'

'Well, do you see the signature at the bottom? The signature of the person who is expecting you to deliver?'

Suddenly a light came on in Bullfrog's head.

'Just so we both know, that is my signature!' Christian said.

Christian brushed him aside and walked past me. 'Ttttt, my boy, let's finish. We, too, have a deadline.'

My master chef and I were very blessed. Our primary task was to feed the main house and look after all the president's guests. As all the VVVVVIPs were getting ready for the banquet, we had time to assist in the banquet preparations where they were trailing – and even to watch the proceedings, at times, when it suited us.

The rest of the prep for the inauguration ran smoothly and everyone was polite to one another.

Once all the contract chefs had been called for their instructions by Mr Bullfrog I-feel-like-an-ass, I stood in the passage outside the kitchen and watched all the dignitaries arrive. That day, you needed clearance even to stand at a window. Fortunately, I could go anywhere I wanted, so I watched how the world came to pay their respects to our new president as one vehicle after the other pulled up, delivering more dignitaries.

After attending the inauguration at the Union Buildings, the dignitaries were making their way to the guesthouse for the banquet. I watched as they were dropped off at the red carpet leading to the tent, their cars queuing all the way down the driveway.

The next moment, a large black limousine drove up, passing all the other cars in the queue. It entered the circle from the right in an anti-clockwise direction, causing a traffic jam. A few well-dressed men – I can only assume they were security as their guns were clearly visible – rushed to the limousine. I heard the guy in front shouting to the others in Afrikaans, '*Fok, ons het vergeet om vir die Amerikaners te sê hulle moet aan die linkerkant bly!* (Fuck, we forgot to tell the Americans to keep left!)'

When the limousine had parked, Hillary Clinton stepped out graciously and headed down the carpet into the inauguration tent. I spent the next half an hour watching the security guys playing Tetris with cars as they tried to unblock the Clinton roadblock.

I was honoured to have been there that day, from daybreak to when they broke down the tent. I saw more dignitaries and celebrities than you'd find in *People* magazine.

I also saw Madiba getting the position and acknowledgement he deserved.

I was there.

4
Meeting the president properly

A FEW DAYS AFTER THE INAUGURATION, we were told that President Mandela was going to stay at the guesthouse for a few days until they had found him a proper residence. Protocol was still not giving us the correct information concerning meals and functions. So, we would count how many people were in the guesthouse and make a call about how much food to prepare and how many staff members to have around for the evening.

That day, there were no cars outside and we could not hear any voices in any of the large rooms, so we decided to call it a day. Christian had already left and I was doing a final sweep of the guesthouse to make sure everything had been locked up before I could also leave. The two of us always worked in shifts, otherwise we would never get any sleep – it was our job to run the guesthouse, be the liaison, greet and welcome all delegates, and look after VIP guests, and we had still to do the cooking.

I had my brogues on and my shirt out as I casually walked down the passage checking everything. I enjoyed the noise my soles made on the marble floors and even broke into a quick tap dance now and then, thinking, *If only my friends could see me now*. I was still taking the events of the past few weeks in, trying to absorb everything and store it in my memory so I would never forget.

Tip tap I went, down the long marble passage. The next thing, I heard a voice: 'Who is there?'

Startled, I looked up. By then, everyone was supposed to have left. I looked around and could see no one.

Again, the voice spoke: 'Who is there?'

Then it hit me – President Mandela was still in the house. The bodyguards had all left, since he was not going anywhere until the next morning. This was standard procedure, since the estate was guarded.

I was gripped by panic. What to do? Until that point, I had only seen President Mandela in passing. Except for the one incident with his family members, I had not been formally introduced, nor had a conversation with him. Quite frankly, I was intimidated.

I ran a few options through my head:

Plan 1: Take off my shoes and run back to the kitchen.

Plan 2: Skittle down the stairs and out the front door and make like I was never there.

Plan 3: Stand dead still and see what happens.

For a few seconds, there was complete silence. Once I'd got my brain and my confidence back, I slowly headed for the doors of the room from which the voice had emanated. I stuck my head in, and there before me was the president, sitting in one of the large, green, floral wingback chairs. Most people would feel like they were in *Alice in Wonderland* when they sat in those huge chairs, but the president sat in it like he owned it.

'Come in here, boy,' he said. I slowly moved forward, not knowing what to do.

'Please enter,' he repeated.

When I reached the president, I just stood there.

'How are you?' he asked.

'I am fine, President Mandela,' I said with a quiver.

'You seem terrified. Why do you look so afraid?' he asked.

In that moment, I did what I have so often done when I'm under pressure: I put my foot squarely in my mouth. Call it nerves, but that's just how it is with me ... my poor wife can attest to this.

'Why have you not killed us?' I blurted out.

The moment those words were out, I wished I could recall them. I wanted to dissolve into thin air and let the winds blow me away.

The president looked at me with a warm, caring face and said, 'If I must live for yesterday, I would rather die today and not see tomorrow. Why would you ask this, boy?'

I immediately started apologising and said I hadn't realised what I was saying. I told him I had the world of respect for him and begged for his forgiveness. In that moment, I had a flashback of my dad and expected the worst.

But the president remained composed, and encouraged me to calm down. He asked me again why I had asked such a question. I explained how many white South Africans had been indoctrinated by the apartheid government through television, radio and newspapers into believing that black South Africans would chase them into the sea if they ever governed. I was worried that the different race groups would turn on one another, as had happened in other countries in Africa.

Madiba didn't entertain my concerns for very long. It was as if he immediately forgave me for lacking worldly knowledge. Instead, he wanted to know whether I was happy working at the guesthouse and was treated fairly, and whether I enjoyed working with him and all his colleagues.

I was completely overwhelmed and grinned from ear to ear. I kept reassuring him that the past few months had been the most memorable and exciting time of my life and that I felt truly blessed. I thanked the president for the opportunity.

'You are thanking me as if you are leaving. Why?' he asked.

I explained that we worked there on contract and that it would expire soon.

'Would you like to stay and continue working here?'

'More than anything in the world, my president,' I said with a sheepish grin.

'Well, we would love to have you with us. I have heard great things about you from my protection guys and what you did for my family when they were not allowed inside the house. I thank you.'

'I am here under Christian, President. He is my mentor.'

'I know, young man. He is staying with us too. The Frenchman is a great man.'

I thanked the president repeatedly and even gave him half a bow as I walked out. My feet had been completely knocked out from under me.

AT THE TIME, I was so excited about being part of the inauguration and walking among kings and queens, presidents and celebrities, that I did not realise that I was also witnessing the ANC building a government from scratch. In the weeks before and after the inauguration, I met a number of key role-players in the ANC.

The ANC was finding its feet in its new position of power, but it was doing so very quickly. New Cabinet ministers, directors general, judges, and so on were appointed. The location for all of this was right there at the guesthouse. Towards the end of May, I could see things starting to settle in the ranks of the ANC. There was definitely less tension in the air and a friendlier atmosphere.

I also met Mary Mxadana, who was responsible for the president's diary and was constantly at his side – from morning till night. You could see that she made the executive decisions. No one would move unless Mary had approved it. She was tall and built like an athlete; her background was gospel music and one could hear her tweet into a tune now and then. I was blessed to have worked with Mary from 1994 to 2000.

Still, initially she was as critical of my presence as Victor, the bodyguard, and others. I had to earn her trust. She would often pop in to the guesthouse after hours to see the president and would find me still working. Whenever she needed help, I was always willing to assist. She soon saw how well I was looking after the president.

This is what my daily routine looked like at the time:

5 a.m.
I arrived at the guesthouse to be met by the bodyguards on the night shift. By now, I was always greeted with a high-five and a huge smile.

8 a.m.
Everyone began to arrive for the day and the dining rooms filled up with ANC stalwarts such as Mathews Phosa, Tokyo Sexwale, Alfred Nzo and Cyril Ramaphosa. I often heard them having discussions about major issues and hatching plans for our country's future. All of this was happening around me.

I was invisible to all and, for the first time in my life, it did not bother me. If the dining room was full, their next-favourite place to have a meeting would be the kitchen. We would fetch two banquet chairs, place them at the stainless-steel table in the kitchen, serve breakfast, and their discussions would simply carry on.

Below, I describe a typical breakfast served at the guesthouse. Now, please remember that all our service was silver. This means the food was plated on large, round and oval solid-silver trays, weighing between ten and fifteen kilograms. The meal was served in waves. The waiters would start by setting plates in front of each person. The next waiter would then collect the tray and serve each guest; the guest would select the items he or she wanted from the tray. The waiters would use two silver spoons as tongs and place the food neatly onto the guest's plate. Once the guest was happy with his or her selection, the final waiter would garnish the plate.

BREAKFAST

Platter 1
Fresh fruit cuts from Limpopo and Mpumalanga

Platter 2
Fifteen-year-old Parma ham

Italian salami

Hungarian gypsy beef

French chafed, smoked beef

Smoked chicken

Stilton cheese

Bergkäse

Brie

Camembert

Provolone

Platter 3
Croque-monsieur

Freshly made baguettes, croissants, rolls and toast

Platter 4
Honeycomb

Homemade preserves

Butter balls

Savoury butter

Fresh berry crush

Platter 5
Macon

Bacon

Beef chipolatas

Health mince

Chafed, sautéed fillet of beef

Platter 6
Bell pepper beans

Sautéed balsamic cherry tomato rosemary skewers

Potato savoury pancakes
Tofu phyllo baskets
Breakfast vegetable quiche
Platter 7
Poached eggs
Fried eggs
Scrambled eggs
Boiled eggs
Scotch eggs

After each course, or platter selection, we would reset a plate and cutlery for the next course.

When we served breakfast, Mary would come down to the kitchen and ask for the president's breakfast. At that time, he had most of his meals in his suite, which had a dining area. I would have a silver tray set out with the cutlery and crockery set according to the meal. An example of what the president would eat for breakfast is a bowl of fresh oats, a plate of fresh fruit, a boiled egg, toast and freshly squeezed orange juice.

Madiba loved healthy, natural foods; he wanted to taste the original flavour of fruits and vegetables. He never liked a sauce over his vegetables; salt and pepper with some butter was all he wanted. We were fortunate that many farmers sent different raw foods as gifts. Whenever I presented a meal made from such donations, I would always tell the president where in the country it came from.

12 p.m.

For lunch, I would serve a three-course meal. It was also silver service, served in waves. These meals would be healthy and quick. The president usually joined his colleagues for lunch in the main dining room. Here is an example of a lunch.

Starters
Halloumi, melon and mint salad with a side order of celery root and homemade mayo

or

French onion soup

Main course
Grilled West Coast sole with cilantro herb butter

or

Entrecôte Mirabeau, with
Pommes Duchesse
Colourful bell pepper basmati terrines
Plum tomatoes filled with caramelised shallots
Fried ginger spinach
Cocktail carrots, steamed and salted, stem on
Courgette ribbons

Dessert
Homemade cream and vanilla pod ice cream
Chocolate mousse
Crème brûlée

Everyone still at the guesthouse by late afternoon would also be served dinner. One day, I was sitting in one of the wingback chairs in the passage, because the dinner prep was ready and the meetings in all the rooms in the guesthouse were going on a bit long.

A gentleman came up to me. I jumped up.

'Pleased to meet you. I am Frank Chikane,' he said in his husky voice (if you closed your eyes you would think you were listening to Barry White).

'Pleased to meet you sir. I am—'

'I know who you are. You're the chef who is looking after all of us. I just wanted to come and thank you. We really appreciate it.'

I had heard that Rev Chikane was one of the regulars in the

passageways of the guesthouse. I had also heard that apartheid security forces had tried to assassinate him in 1989. It had come up one night when I was talking to the bodyguards, who had great respect for him because he was so kind and forgiving. As one of them said, had he been in Rev Chikane's shoes he would've hated the person who tried to kill him for the rest of his life. But not Rev Chikane – he was a true Christian.

I stood up and thanked the reverend for his compliments. I decided to ask him a question I'd always been curious about. 'Sir, may I ask you something?'

'Yes,' he said.

'People have tried to assassinate you. Are you fine with it now?'

He laughed. 'I have always had someone look over me. I believe He will continue to look over me.'

I excused myself to help Christian finish preparing supper. As I walked into the kitchen, Mary was looking in the pots and soaking up the aromas. She would usually have a quick bite, because she had to take care of the president while everyone else was eating, and would only eat later.

Then, 'Christian, I would like to ask you something,' she said. 'President Mandela will be staying at the guesthouse for quite a while and I would like to ask you and the chef to stay on. Would that be fine with you?'

Christian, charming as ever, turned around and said it would be our honour. 'Madam, we would, however, need a few things to change. Things must be more transparent. We would need our own budget and we must be allowed to run the guesthouse as is expected.'

Mary smiled and said, 'Yes, just tell me what you need.'

When she'd left, Christian went to the wine fridge, and grabbed a great bottle of white wine and two crystal glasses. He poured them to the brim, and knocked his back. I followed suit; we filled the glasses again, and knocked those back, too.

'Okay – enough now. Supper is not going to cook itself,' Christian said as he took off his suit jacket and put on his chef's jacket.

Here is an example of the dinners we would serve – again, silver service.

Starters
Almond grilled trout
or
Cheese soufflé

Main course
Kingklip Grenobloise
or
Vienna schnitzel with gratin dauphinois, with
Fluffed butter mash
South African French carved root vegetables

Dessert
Banane Martiniquaise
Croquembouche

My team at the Presidential Guesthouse. Christian Michel is standing to the left of Mandela. I am on Mandela's right.

After going through the same routine for about a month and seeing the same faces, things slowly became more stable and organised. Everyone, including the staff at the guesthouse, was finding their feet. By the end of May, it was mostly the upper echelons of the ANC and the members of the new Government of National Unity, including those from the National Party, who visited the guesthouse most regularly.

One evening, I walked into the dining room to find the entire top structure of the ANC sitting there. One of them, a minister, turned to me and asked me to join them. I thanked him, but said I was there to serve them and ensure that dinner ran smoothly.

When his colleagues repeated the invitation, I went and got myself a plate of food and sat down at the table. The minister explained to me that the ANC operated as a family. During the day, when there was work to be done, everyone was focused – there was no time for play and everyone knew their place in the ranks. Yet, after hours, the ANC came together as comrades and friends – as a family.

I sat there looking at all these great men. Many had lost years of their life serving prison sentences during apartheid. They'd lost loved ones and sacrificed more than anyone who has not been in their position could ever understand. This team of admirable men, this family, was going to take our country into the new era. I was convinced they could unite us.

The mere fact that they could appreciate what I did, and that they believed every single person counted – no matter where they fitted into the scheme of things and regardless of their colour, religion or creed – showed me that they were committed to the dream of a democratic South Africa where every person and group would be respected.

I was incredibly honoured to sit at that table that night. I would like to mention all the ministers of President Mandela's Cabinet, because I met them all and each played a major role that should never be forgotten.

NELSON MANDELA (President), Thabo Mbeki (Deputy President), FW de Klerk (Deputy President), Kraai van Niekerk (Agriculture), Derek Hanekom (Agriculture and Land Affairs), Thoko Msane-Didiza (Deputy Minister of Agriculture) Ben Ngubane (Arts, Culture, Science and Technology), Sipo Mzimela (Correctional Services), Joe Modise (Defence), Sibusiso Bengu (Education), Dawie de Villiers and Bantu Holomisa (Minister and Deputy Minister of Environmental Affairs and Tourism), Derek Keys (Finance), Gill Marcus (Deputy Minister of Finance from 1996), Alfred Nzo and Aziz Pahad (Minister and Deputy Minister of Foreign Affairs), Nkosazana Dlamini-Zuma (Health), Chief Mangosuthu Buthelezi (Home Affairs), Joe Slovo (Housing), Dullah Omar (Justice), Tito Mboweni (Labour), Pik Botha (Minerals and Energy), Pallo Jordan (Posts, Telecommunications and Broadcasting), Roelf Meyer and Valli Moosa (Minister and Deputy Minister of Provincial Affairs and Constitutional Development), Stella Sigcau (Public Enterprises), Zola Skweyiya (Public Service and Administration), Jeff Radebe (Public Works), Sidney Mufamadi (Safety and Security), Steve Tshwete (Sport and Recreation), Trevor Manuel (Trade and Industry and Minister of Finance from 1996), Mac Maharaj (Transport), Kader Asmal (Water Affairs and Forestry), Abe Williams (Welfare and Population Development) and Jay Naidoo (minister without portfolio).

5
Moving in with Madiba

At the end of June, the guesthouse's west wing opened up and I was asked to move into it with my family. By now, I was a son richer, so I was elated: it had three bedrooms, a lounge, a huge kitchen, a pantry and – best of all – it was probably the safest place in the country.

Just when I thought things could not get better, they delivered a Kombi, a bakkie and two upmarket sedans to be used for guesthouse operations. At this stage, the president was out of the country so we had time to move in and get settled. I was also in constant communication with Mary, so I was kept in the loop about the latest guesthouse developments.

The west wing was enormous. We had three large bedrooms, a storeroom, a massive bathroom, a guest toilet, a large kitchen with a balcony overlooking the other houses on the estate, and an incredible lounge – fireplace and all.

Outside the lounge was the roof of the Banquet Hall, which we quietly made our front garden. Not in the gardening sense – but we braaied on the roof, played games there, and so on. From the roof, we had a view of most of Pretoria. We partied where many people would drool about merely seeing.

So, Tracey and I moved in. We had got engaged quickly and would tie the knot soon afterwards: this beauty was not going to get away from me. She was, and still is, my princess.

A few days later, a message was sent to all the management teams who worked in the Departments of Foreign Affairs and Finance, at the guesthouse and the embassy desk, that there would be an urgent meeting the following day. Mary had called the meeting. Since she was the president's right hand and managed his diary, she was tasked with assisting the Department of Foreign Affairs. It was as if Mary was the liaison between the world and President Mandela – people only got to him through Mary.

Rumours flew that heads were going to roll. I arrived at the Department's office in Hilda Street in Hatfield. A group of about fifty people was standing around outside a boardroom, waiting to be called in for the meeting. Since Christian had been appointed on a contract basis, he did not have to attend.

I was called over by someone who was part of the old guard. 'Have you heard, Chef?' he said.

'No, heard what?'

'Apparently all the whites are being fired.'

I was immediately upset by his tone. 'You are talking nonsense. That's just another rumour.'

Since I didn't want to listen to any more of that kind of talk, I moved away to a window until we were called in.

As one of the directors walked out of the boardroom, he looked at the crowd of mostly whites and gave a whistle, the kind you hear in a Western just before the head honcho shoots down a whole group of baddies. In all honesty, when we stepped into the boardroom my ass was chewing on my underpants like someone who is trying to stop smoking chews on gum.

I had done my job well, I thought, and had been through so much in the past few months. I didn't want to lose it all. But with all the changes in the government, and the levels of transformation required, anything was possible.

Mary then stood up and started telling us that she was disappointed in some of us and that yes, some people would be asked to leave. Firstly, she was very upset that some Foreign Affairs officials apparently did not attend scheduled meetings at foreign embassies and did not even have the decency to let the embassy officials know they weren't coming.

Okay, on this point I'm fine, I thought. Whenever I'd been called to a meeting at the guesthouse, I'd attended.

Secondly, Mary pointed out that time-sensitive responses were not dealt with timeously and that, by 4:30 p.m, the offices of Foreign Affairs officials were often empty. No one was willing to work a minute past their official office hours to get the job done and help us towards a new South Africa.

Once again, I was not the one in trouble: I worked for about sixteen hours a day.

When she got to the third point, Mary was visibly upset. 'Some of you attend functions or meetings and act like you are the VIPs. I have received reports of people in this boardroom who drink while they are on duty and even take an invited guest's seat.'

I knew exactly who Mary was taking about. In a few instances, I'd had to ask some of them to stand up so I could seat a dignitary – and then even got attitude from them.

Mary started reading out names, and asked those named to stand up. My name was called. We were asked to stand on one side of the room, still not knowing whether we'd been fired. This group was about fifteen per cent white and twenty-five per cent Indian, with the remaining members being black people.

Then, the others were asked to stand up. Mary informed them that they'd been fired and should go straight to Human Resources. I nearly gave the person next to me a high-five: I was that relieved.

While most of the group that had been dismissed were white, there were a few black employees among them. As they filed out sullenly, one of the black gentlemen turned around, looked Mary straight in the face and said, 'What's wrong with you? I am black!'

Mary remained composed and said, 'Sorry, sir, do I look green to you? I am also black, but I've grabbed the opportunities offered to me to further myself. For this reason, I am your boss. In this government, only hard work and dedication will get you anywhere – not the colour of your skin.'

If I'd ever doubted it, I now knew exactly who I was working for. My chain of command was simple – Mary, then the president. I went back to the guesthouse, opened a bottle of champagne and celebrated another milestone in my career.

THE FOLLOWING DAY, Mary came around and gave me my first-ever cellphone. It was huge: I thought it might have a slot to put coins in! But, jokes aside, I was honoured to have one as I had only read and heard about this new piece of equipment that was just then hitting the world.

I asked Mary where the phones came from. She said Vodacom had given them to the Presidency. 'One is for me, one is for the president, and the rest are for the people we need to keep in contact with. Don't ever turn it off, and keep it with you all the time.'

I'm sure she could see from the look on my face that I felt like a kid in a candy store.

Later that day, my new cellphone rang. I first did a quick dance around it to celebrate, then looked around to see if anyone else was listening. To my grave disappointment, it was only me.

'Hello, Chef Brett here at the Presidential Guesthouse. How may I help you?'

'*Wa gafa* (You're crazy), it's Mary!'

'Hello, my lady, how may I help you?'

'Tata is coming back later this afternoon. Make food for him and make sure his room is ready. I will inform him that you are waiting for him.'

'Yes, my lady,' I said, not knowing that this brick of a phone would change the way we communicate forever.

I asked the chambermaids to go upstairs and we polished the stairs, passages and every item again. We made sure every light bulb was clean in every polished chandelier, and working.

I went into the president's suite and checked that everything was perfect. Fresh fruit display: check (I could even see my face in the apples). Mineral waters all turned the right way: check. Crystal glasses sparkling as the sunlight shone on them: check.

The following gives an idea of the routine on the president's arrival. I would get a message from our security team at the front door that the president was five minutes away. I would then go downstairs in my suit and wait on the red carpet, hands behind my back, feet together, cologne on to hide the smell of the food I'd been making, and the reflection from my shiny shoes lighting up my face.

We would hear over the two-way radio that the president's convoy had just entered the main gate in Church Street. First, the motorcycles would come racing up like greyhounds around the track corner. The cars would follow, with their V6 engines.

Under the leadership of Eddie Meiring, the front cars would pass and the middle car, a Mercedes-Benz S600, would stop at exactly the right place with the door perfectly aligned with the red carpet. Now, let me first tell you about Eddie: he was a judo expert and highly trained in combat and VVIP protection. He was one of those types who could probably kill a man with a blade of grass. He had many years' experience; in my eyes, he was the best in the industry. Tata also adored him.

Once the car had stopped, Eddie would jump out of the front passenger seat, look around (I still believe bodyguards work more on instinct than on sight) and give a signal. The next moment, the rest of the security team would get out of the cars, their brute energy palpable, and take their positions. They all had designated places to stand to protect the president.

Then, the president's door would finally open and he would get out.

'How are you, young man?' he'd always ask when he saw me.

I would turn around to lead the president into the guesthouse. We would take the stairs to the top landing, with the president leaning on me. I will never forget those brief walks. From there, I would rush to the lift between the office and reception, hold it open, catch the lift up to the top floor with him, and escort him to his suite.

'May I fetch your tea now, President?'

'Yes please. If you don't mind, I will have it in the room.'

I would go down to the kitchen, which was a mere sixty metres from the president's suite. With a whistle on my lips and a wag in my tail, I'd fetch one cup and one saucer, give each a quick wipe to ensure it was clean, polish the teaspoon, turn it around to look at my distorted face (of course, a chuckle would follow), then prepare a pot of boiling water with two rooibos tea bags, put some organic honey in a small jar with another teaspoon, and place it all on a mirror-clean silver tray with a crisp, white doily.

Then, off I'd go upstairs. As I'd get close to the room, I would put down the tray, wipe my shoes on the back of my pants, and straighten my tie and jacket. I'd knock on the door.

'President, I have your tea ready.'

Then, that deep, soothing voice would ask me to enter. I'd put a chair in one corner of the main room, where the light was perfect for the president to sit and read. I'd also put a side table there, on which I'd put his tea.

'Here is your tea, President. Would you like dinner at 6:30?'

'Thank you, that would be nice. Please may I eat in the Breakfast Room?'

'That will be done, President. I will come and fetch you just before.'

As I'd walk out, I'd always get a 'thank you'.

I would then go downstairs and ask Phineas, the maître d', to set a table for one in the Breakfast Room, and start the prep for dinner.

On the day of that first cellphone call, I had received fresh, whole Karoo lambs and cut up the carcasses, so I knew I could use lamb for mains. We'd had a farmer send the most beautiful tomatoes earlier that day, so I had to use them – I knew the president would enjoy what I made from the produce of a man who had gone to that much trouble.

As the president ate healthily, I would take fruit from around our country and make a pretty display with it. I would also make some ice cream and place a small dish of it at the centre of the fruit display, just in case the president was tempted.

I placed a double boiler on the stove for the ice cream and added a litre of fresh cream. I then took a vanilla pod and cut it in half, and pressed down on the flesh with a knife to push the oils and flavours out. With the same knife, I scraped up all the seeds and the flesh, and added them to the cream. I left it to reduce by half. (I never add sugar at this stage – doing so means that you start with a sweet, creamy mixture and end with a yellowish sugar syrup that is only good for diabetes. Adding sugar only once the cream has reduced gives the perfect taste. How much? Simple: according to your taste.)

I then started on the vegetables. I peeled some baby carrots with the stems on, making them all exactly the same size, and washed some courgettes before slicing them in five-centimetre segments. Crap – I'd forgotten to put the water on for the rice, so I did that. With my paring knife, I cleaned the courgettes' sides so they each resembled a pencil, then sorted the green beans so that they were all similar in girth and length. I cut them all exactly the same length, and then in half. They had to be perfect: they were for my president. I placed them neatly on a cutting board and covered them with a clean, damp cloth.

Then, I went to the cold rooms downstairs for my lamb chops in their vacuum bag, nicely sealed to mature the meat and keep it sterile. I ran upstairs, took them out and washed them, and placed them on a separate cutting board with a damp cloth. I added the rice to the boiling water.

Over in the veg room, I chose six of the farmer's tomatoes, washed them in the veg sink, and placed five of them in a bowl of boiling water. While the skin was wilting off the meat of the tomatoes, I was thoroughly enjoying the sixth one. It was *so* divine. I washed my hands and pulled the skin off the tomatoes.

A lot of the ways in which I made food for the president were different from what you might expect. There was a reason for this: the president was blessed in that many people around the world took a lot of time to ensure that he stayed healthy. I'd been taught by doctors, professors, dieticians and the president's family and friends, people who loved him. So, I cooked to please the president and his health, so the world would have the privilege of having him around forever. When the Banting diet, and all the others, came out – diets that only got names years later – I had been cooking in a similar way since 1994. What I learnt at the guesthouse truly affected my cooking style and all my recipes. Healthy, tasty and beautiful, all wrapped up into one awesome meal, with my secret ingredients – love and passion.

Okay, back to my cooking. I diced the tomatoes, placed them in a pan at a low temperature with butter, and slowly fried them until the moisture dissipated. Then, I added a bit of fresh basil, salt and pepper. Sea salt, obviously; and yes, we did use margarine – to grease the door locks and latches. That's all it's good for. Once the herbs and spices had sautéed into the tomatoes, I added boiling water to make a soup. I watched for the natural oil of the tomatoes to start forming on top of the water, my tell-tale sign that they were almost ready.

I placed the carrots and beans into the steamer. After several minutes, I added the courgettes. Then, 'Oh, crap – the rice!' I ran over and grabbed the pot.

On the solid-top stove, everything was hot.

I ran to the sink, just making it before dropping the pot. That was bright, as what little of the hot water that was left had spat out of the pot and burnt me further. You must remember that if I were elegant, I would be an accountant, lawyer or engineer.

I found a cloth and poured the rice into a colander. (Here are some tips for making rice. First, don't forget it! Next, cook in until it is al dente. Then, place it back into the pot after draining it in the colander, turn the stove off and place the pot on back on the stove, covered with a cloth. Leave it to steam – this will make it light and fluffy.)

Then, it was back to the ice cream. I added the sugar into the cream that had reduced and thickened, making it taste *amazing*. I passed the mixture through some cheesecloth, straight into the ice cream machine.

I took my veg out of the steamer and placed them into a dish, poured melted butter over them, and seasoned them with salt and pepper, and just a pinch of brown malt sugar for the carrots. I covered them with foil. Then I took a cloth – see, I learnt from the rice pot: to be born stupid we can all accept, but to die stupid is extremely sad. I fetched the tomato soup as the tomato oils were starting to show on the water, and voorvoored it. A voorvoor is a blender, in my language. To me, a blender does not go 'blend, blend, blend'. If it makes that sound, it's time to throw it away. A blender goes 'voor, voor, voor' – hence, it's a voorvoor machine.

Once voorvoored, the soup went back into the pot. When it came to the boil, I slowly added cream while whisking vigorously, leaving a bit of cream for garnish. Then I turned down the heat and added sea salt and pepper to taste.

Next, I took three ramekin dishes and coated them with butter.

I put the rice, with salt and pepper, into the ramekin dishes and pushed it down, then added a blob of butter and wrapped each one with cling wrap.

We always would make flavoured butters at the guesthouse. We whisked the butter until it was fluffy, lightly salted it as it was salted butter (lesson learnt – trust me – when I almost made an anchovy), then added herbs as one flavour, paprika as another, saffron as another, and so on. We then wrapped each flavoured batch in plastic wrap and ensured that each made a cylinder shape.

Why do I tell you this? Because I was starting the lamb chops now. The president was never a great lover of gravy, but all meat and fish needs a bit of flavour. So, I would serve different butters with his meals, which would vary their taste.

With a sharp knife, I made a cut in the chops just above the fillet on the bone, then scraped all the meat and sinew off the bone until it was white. Then, I wiped the bone with lemon juice and wrapped it in foil, to keep the bone white during cooking. I spiced the oil in the pan with sea salt and pepper, and waited for it to start smoking. I placed the lamb chops into the hot oil and browned them on both sides.

Once both sides were brown, I rubbed butter onto a tray and placed the lamb chops on a dry cloth to get rid of the excess oil. I then placed them on the tray with a bit of butter on top of them, so when I heated them up they would stay moist.

The reason I cooked like this at the guesthouse is that we never knew when things were going to happen. The president could have a meeting scheduled for an hour that could take three; or, the meeting could take all of ten minutes and everyone would want to eat right away, before the next session. So, at any given time, we could have eight to ten minutes to start serving. Through experience, I became able to prep fresh food, full of goodness and taste, that I could serve on demand.

(The biggest event I catered for was 25 000 people over seven days, three times a day – plated, just to top it off. Have you got any friggen idea what it's like to break 75 000 eggs every morning? I did quite a few 10 000-person functions for President Mandela around our beautiful country – three- to five-course breakfasts, lunches or dinners. I made like a hunter, and ate each elephant bite by bite – I would cater for 100 people at a time; so, if a function was for 4 000 people, I would treat it as 40 times 100 people.)

But back to serving the president. I took a brief run along the passage, up the wooden stairs and along the upstairs passage, and made a quick left, to the door to the president's room.

Knock, knock, knock. 'Evening, President. Supper is ready. Would you like me to bring it up, or would you like to come down to the Breakfast Room?'

'I will be down now.'

'Would you like me to wait and assist you, President?'

'No thank you, going downstairs is fine. Just help me when I come up again.'

'Will do, President. See you now-now,' I said, and ran downstairs again.

As Phineas signalled me, I met the president in the passage and escorted him into the Breakfast Room. Once I had told the president what the menu was, and poured him a glass of fresh water, I ran to the kitchen, Phineas standing ready halfway through the door.

I took a warm bowl out of the oven and placed it on a doily plate, ladled fresh soup into it, made a cream design on top with a dollop of stiffer whipped cream, then placed a fresh basil sprig on the cream. At a wave of my hand, Phineas came and collected it on a silver tray. I joined the president then.

'My president, I have made a fresh, healthy tomato soup. A farmer sent you fresh tomatoes from his farm as a gift. They were incredible, so I used them.'

'Very nice, I must say. Please would you convey my appreciation to the farmer?'

'I will do, President. You will make his day. I will send a letter on our Presidential Guesthouse letterhead.'

I went back to the kitchen to start warming up the dinner and serve the president his favourite dish, followed by dessert.

ONE NIGHT, I was busy serving the president dinner while Mary was discussing his calendar with him. His cellphone rang. We all looked at each other, a bit startled – this did not really happen. In fact, it never happened. Mary walked over to the table on which it was lying and picked it up.

'Hello, Mary Mxadana here, aide to the president.'

I heard someone speaking on the other side. Eventually, Mary gave the phone to the president. I heard the whole conversation. Then, the president handed the phone back to Mary and asked her to give the gentleman the banking details, which she did.

A while later, while I was clearing the table to bring the president his rooibos tea, the phone rang again. This time, we were all cool about it. Again, Mary took the call. She looked at the president and confirmed that the president wanted to give the gentleman on the line the banking details for the Nelson Mandela Children's Fund. You must know that the gentleman on the line was, and still is, a prominent businessman internationally. Mary politely asked him if she could phone him back – you could hear that he was extremely upset about something.

Mary turned to the president and informed him that the gentleman wanted to give a donation to the president personally, and not just to 'some charity'. The president looked at us, astonished, and said, 'If the gift is for me, then it is for me to use as I please, and all gifts to me will go to my fund for the children to enjoy. I don't take money.

Please tell him that, if he is unhappy, he can reverse the payment!'

Mary picked up the phone and conveyed the message. She was firm – I am sure the caller got the message, loud and clear.

I walked back to the kitchen, so proud to have been privy to what had just happened. My president – our president – could not be bribed, and had become even greater in my eyes (I didn't think this was possible). All the money he received he gave back to the country through the children – the country's future.

As the days and weeks went by, I was blessed to spend more and more time with the president after hours. I could not absorb his lessons quickly enough. When he had surgery for cataracts in July 1994, I was asked to help with his eyedrops and change his dressing when required at night. I checked up on him regularly after the operation, and we got closer. He also had a knee that troubled him. I would rub muscle gel onto it and assist him with his knee brace. The president was human – hard to believe, I know.

Some nights, I could hear the president walking around. I would always ask if I could assist him in any way. He was always so polite, and would just smile and say he was stretching his legs. I would always insist that he was welcome in our section at any time – no invitation required.

One evening, when the president returned from Luthuli House, ANC headquarters, Mary told me that no dinner was required as he'd had a large lunch. So, I welcomed him on his arrival back at the guesthouse, walking him up the first flight of stairs and to the lift as I always did. I made him his rooibos tea, and asked whether there would be anything else. He told me that he wanted to rest, so I went to the wing of the guesthouse where we stayed.

I put on a pair of PT shorts and my old, worn Pretoria Boys High T-shirt, its history of touch rugby on the front lawn and sneaking out of the hostel to go swimming at night clearly marked in holes.

I finished making my son's favourite – macaroni and cheese –

and started doing his homework with him. I sat at the kitchen table getting irritated with my five-year-old, who was more interested in the pigeons pooping outside on the windowsill than his work. I heard a knock on the door, which I ignored; the door was always open so I could hear what was happening in the guesthouse. The next thing, I heard that voice – the one that sounded like it came from heaven.

'The young man is not interested as you are explaining it the wrong way.'

I jumped off my chair and nearly knocked the president right off his feet.

'Sorry, President. I did not see you there.'

'Am I interfering at all?'

'No, President, it is our honour to have you in our house.'

The president chuckled. 'We live together under one roof, so it's all our house.'

'So true, President, which shows that you are always welcome.'

My wife walked past and greeted the president, then went down the passage to drop off our washing.

'May I assist with the homework?'

Keagan sat there, grinning, as if he already knew that this man far outranked his dad. A while later I went to the lounge to lay the table for dinner and my wife joined me. It amused us that our son didn't realise how great the man was who was teaching him. Later, we called Keagan and the president for dinner. As we sat down, the president sat on the couch to watch TV – he truly was not hungry.

Keagan whined about the president not wanting to eat. After we'd prayed, I asked him if he knew who the president was.

'*Daaaaad*,' he answered.

I asked him again.

'Yes, Dad. That is Tata.'

I immediately raised my voice: 'No, that is President Mandela.'

'Chef, please,' the president said, 'Keagan and I have chatted often. When I walk around the guesthouse, he often comes to speak to me. We have great talks, don't we, Keagan?'

Keagan smiled and nodded.

'So that's where you go when we can't find you …'

'Sorry, Daddy.'

I gave Keagan a huge hug and reassured him that, for as long as he stayed in the guesthouse, he'd be in the safest place in the world.

Later that night, the president excused himself and went back to his wing. His visits started becoming regular. Needless to say, we loved it.

The next day, we had a state visit lunch in the Banquet Hall, so I spent the day prepping the food and setting up. When everything was ready, I went upstairs for a quick shower and put a suit on.

I welcomed all the guests who came down the Banquet Hall walkway. Once all the guests were seated, I fetched the president from the Pink Room. As we were about to enter the Banquet Hall, Keagan came running up to us, shouting at the top of his voice: 'Daddy! Tata! Daddy! Tata!'

I slowed down and tried to shoo him away. We were right in front of the Banquet Hall doors, and everyone could see us. The guests were burning to see the president; the media behind us were waiting to capture another photograph of him.

I tried to push my son to one side, using gestures to show him to run upstairs. The next thing, the president turned around to look.

Great. Here we go, I thought. *Another cock-up in my life. Back to Mary's office to get kicked out of the department and embarrassed. Like, why did you get fired? Oh, my son ran amok at a banquet at the Presidential Guesthouse.*

'Hello, Keagan! What is the great news?'

Keagan was jumping up and down like a Jack Russell that had just chased and caught its first bus out on the street. 'Look! Look! Look!'

he yelled, pointing at his head. On his head was a gold star – at that age, he must have felt like an actor who'd just won an Oscar.

I could feel everyone's eyes on me; the cameras flashed from all sides. Oh, I wanted to look, all right – I wanted to look with a slap on his butt.

The photo that appeared in the newspapers when my son rushed up to show President Mandela his gold star.

'Chef, look at what he did and stop looking so concerned,' the president said, as if that is what I was worried about. Meanwhile, I was waving goodbye to my career. It seemed that the president was just as pleased with himself that *his* teaching Keagan about the colours of the rainbow had earned Keagan his gold star. I think we had the most famous tutor in the world.

He turned to me. 'Take the young man upstairs and congratulate him. He did well. I will wait for you.'

Needless to say, I did the hundred-metre dash in 3,2 seconds and got straight back to the president. As I walked him into the Banquet Hall, he said under his breath, 'Don't worry. He is just a child. You see, I taught him well!'

That is how great a man he was.

The following day, the reporter who covered the story for a national Sunday newspaper brought me a photo that captured this moment. The great man cared for all people, no matter who they were.

6
'Life seems to work things out for us'

If memory serves me correctly, it was the beginning of June 1997. President Mandela was on an Asian trip, so I knew I'd have a few days free for some personal running around.

Prior to his leaving, he asked me to research body language and how it had the potential to offend people of other cultures. He knew I'd done a bit of self-study on this topic, as we had discussed it on one of our casual nights.

I was standing in the queue in the Standard Bank in Pretoria's Brooklyn Mall when my cellphone rang. I took it out of my pocket and saw 'Big Boss Tata' on my screen.

I knew that, by the time I made it out of the bank, it would be too late to take the call. So, I decided to answer the phone in the bank, knowing full well it was not permitted.

I slowly shrunk down in the queue, my head just below that of the people in front of me and behind me, like a buck on the plains blending in with the long, dry grass and hoping not to be seen.

'Great day to you, Tata, how can I help you?' I said in a low voice, trying to avoid alerting the hunters.

'Hello, Chef. How are you? But first, why are you whispering?'

'Sorry, Tata. Is that better?'

'Oh,' I heard on the phone, 'but who are you speaking to?'

I got the feeling that I was insulting the president, so I let the fear fall away and all the stares bounce off.

'Yes – my president,' I said, louder.

'President who, my boy?'

'President Mandela of South Africa.'

The line went quiet. All I could hear was my own breathing. Then, I heard a gentle chuckle on the other side.

'You are standing in a crowd at the moment, are you not?'

'Yes, President Mandela, I am in the bank.'

'Don't you feel silly? I bet everyone thinks you are crazy!'

'You are absolutely right, President!'

'I was only joking with you. Please phone Mary when you can. I just want to ask you something about the discussion we had the other night. Thank you, Chef.'

'Thank you, President, I will. Speak to you later.'

I could imagine the looks I was getting and the sniggers behind my back, but I did not care. Every time I looked up and saw someone glancing at me, I laughed.

As I got to the counter, the beautiful African woman behind the glass did not know how to handle me and my laughing.

'How may I help you today?' she asked, unsure.

'Please may I pay this money into my account?' I replied, passing her my bank card and ID book.

The teller started processing my request on the computer. Then, she paused and looked up at me. 'Your physical address is the Presidential Guesthouse of South Africa in Bryntirion Estate?'

'Yes, my lady. That is where I live.'

Her face lit up like fire. 'So that *was* the president on the line?'

'Yes, my lady.'

'You know everyone thinks you're mad.'

'I know, but I just don't care!'

ON THE PRESIDENT'S RETURN from Asia, life got back to normal and we resumed our routines. One morning, he had to leave early for an appointment. By 6 a.m., we had him fed and ready. As he was walking to the car, he paused and looked at his personal security detail.

'Eddie, have all of you eaten?'

'No, Mr President. We will have something once we have dropped you off.'

He turned to me. 'Chef, could you feed these strong men before I leave? They have come all the way here so early in the morning.'

'Yes, President. It won't take long at all.'

'I know it is early, but no one should go to work hungry.'

'Yes, President. I'll get onto it immediately.'

I walked him up the stairs, and assisted him to the Pink Room. Eddie came up behind us in the passage.

'Mr President, are you not going to be late?'

'Don't you worry, Eddie. I will inform Mary.'

As I worked long hours with the bodyguards, we had all become a family. Under Eddie Meiring, the unit ran like clockwork. If I remember correctly, he was the first white bodyguard in the presidential unit.

The bodyguards all came upstairs and joined me in the kitchen, where they used to eat. I had security at the front door protect the house so the bodyguards could all eat at once.

As I was making their food and they were helping themselves to it, the camaraderie and unanimous praise for the president were beautiful.

It did not take long. As one bodyguard after another finished his meal, I got a high-five or a thank-you pat on the back before they all ran downstairs. I went to fetch the president from the Pink Room and escorted him down to the front door.

He climbed into his Mercedes-Benz, and all the bodyguards jumped into their assigned cars. Eddie stood outside the lead car's passenger door. Once everyone was in and he was happy for the convoy to depart, I got a half smile and wink. He jumped in. Seconds later, they were out of sight.

My president – so human.

ONE MORNING, I was slowly waking up to get dressed: the bed was warm, and my wife was lying in it like Sleeping Beauty, with me admiring her. I heard loud voices up and down the passages, bordering on panic. I got dressed like Flash Gordon and ran down the stairs.

'Eddie, where is Eddie?'

He came around the corner, looking distressed. 'Where is the president? Where is he?'

'In his room. I checked his schedule last night and he is only departing at nine this morning.'

'He is not there! Mary has just jumped down our throats!'

'No man, Eddie. Have you asked the security detail in front?'

'Of course! They are just waiting for one of their unit members to return to question him.'

We ran down the passage, then down the stairs to the room by the front door where the unit was stationed twenty-four hours a day.

'Radio your member and see where he is. NOW!'

The leader of the unit raised the member on the radio.

'Ja, Sergeant. I can hear you,' came the response.

'Constable, we have a situation. Where are you?'

'I am walking with the president around the grounds, like I do every morning.'

'What? Why?' the sergeant asked in utter confusion. You could see boiling point being reached in all the security standing around. The security detail allocated to the guesthouse would protect the president until he stepped outside. Then, he became the responsibility of his personal security detail.

The constable replied warily, 'Sergeant, I do this every morning. The president walks to thank every police officer at each post for looking after him that day.'

'Well, how far are you?'

President Mandela on his daily stroll to thank all the security personnel for protecting him.

'The president is greeting and thanking the last police officer on the north corner near the pool. Then we will be heading back.'

As we stood at the door, we could see the pair approaching, the constable walking behind the president. Eddie and some of his guards walked briskly to the president, formed a circle around him, and escorted him back into the guesthouse.

Once the president was in the Breakfast Room and had started eating, all the bodyguards and the guesthouse security unit pounced on the constable like hyenas that had not eaten in weeks.

'Wait! Wait! Wait!' he screamed as if one of the bodyguards already had his balls in his vice-grip hands. 'Sergeant, please! Help me here! I was following the president's instructions! He told me not to alarm anyone and asked if I could follow him around. There were police officers stationed every fifty metres, so he was never in danger. I was just following the president's instructions!'

Botes, the sergeant, walked up to the constable and stood alongside him. Regardless of his rank, Botes weighed in at about a hundred and twenty kilograms of pure beef and had been in the police for over twenty years. He had a lot of say. 'If he was following instructions, leave him.'

Just like that, the hyenas turned tail and went back to their posts.

People ask me all the time: was President Mandela as great as everyone says he was? The answer is no – he was greater. Name another world leader who would do something like this.

Needless to say, the president's security detail shifts and times changed that day. Every morning, at 5 a.m., there would be two bodyguards at the front door waiting for his morning walk. On the days when he did not go for a walk, he would make his convoy stop on the way out of the estate to allow him to thank each police officer.

Wow, I tell you. Wow.

I RECEIVED NOTIFICATION that there would be a large meeting in the Banquet Hall the following day, hosted by Roelf Meyer. All the Cabinet ministers were expected to attend.

That night, we set up the hall and got the whole guesthouse ready.

We knew that the president would have breakfast and that delegates would then start arriving. There would be meetings between different delegates in the ground-floor rooms. Each room was prepped for teas, coffees and fresh snacks to be brought in as the delegates arrived.

We went through all the rooms, ensuring that they were clean and ready. I locked up and went past the president's room. Everything looked perfect; I went to bed.

The following morning, I beat all the birds. I even beat the sun. I was downstairs opening up, unlocking, greeting all the security who were arriving, and getting my team onto their tasks, ready to look after our government.

Once everything had been prepped, I got the dog unit in to do a sweep from the guesthouse to the Banquet Hall. Then came the debuggers, to ensure the discussions would go no further than the rooms in which they'd be held.

After I'd served the president, I escorted him to the Pink Room, his favourite room to relax or have meetings in. I fetched him his tea and left; Mary would take over the proceedings from then on. I went to the front door to welcome all the dignitaries to the guesthouse and have security escort them to the rooms they would meet in prior to the main meeting in the Banquet Hall.

Once everyone was in and the meetings were under way, I popped in and out of the rooms to check on the refreshments and make sure that nothing else was required. As I walked down the passage, I saw the Pink Room door open, so I took a gap and ran in to freshen everything up. 'Sorry, President. Don't mean to bother you. Are you fine, or do you require anything else?'

'Deputy President De Klerk is arriving soon. Please would you ask him to join me here before we need to go through to Roelf Meyer?'

'With pleasure, President. I will go and wait for him at the front door,' I said, and headed that way.

As the guards at the gate radioed the front-door unit when guests arrived, I stood speaking to Botes and some of the others, having a laugh at their nicknames.

Then: 'Guesthouse, guesthouse, come in.'

'Send to guesthouse.'

'Deputy President De Klerk on the way up.'

'Copy, over.'

So, I went to stand at the door and soon saw the convoy move onto the red carpet. The deputy president got out of his car, discussing a matter with another minister who had got out on the other side.

The deputy president's bodyguards stood in formation awaiting him. I was gently escorted to stand inside the foyer. After several minutes, he started walking towards the foyer, still in discussion. Once he was inside and had stopped speaking, I stepped forward to convey the message from the president to him.

'Morning, Deput—'

Bam! An elbow struck me on my nose. There was pain, and blood in my mouth; my eyes streamed with tears. I got such a fright that I quickly wiped my face with my sleeve just so I could see what was happening. I could only just make out the bodyguard who had hit me as he came for me again. I tried to find the deputy president, but all I could see were his bodyguards. I turned and walked upstairs to my flat so I could change, ego bruised, nose throbbing and blood gushing.

As I walked into the kitchen passage, some of my team members ran up to me to ask if I was okay. As Vincent, one of the chefs in my team, tried to wipe my face with a dishcloth, I decided, *Screw this*. I turned back and walked towards the Pink Room. Just before the deputy president's bodyguards escorted him in, I slipped into the room. I stood between the couches and the settee table and announced, 'President Mandela, the deputy president has arrived.'

'Chef! What happened to you?'

'Sorry, President. I awaited the deputy president as per your instructions. When he arrived, I stepped forward to convey your message and one of the bodyguards struck me in the face.'

The deputy president, who was now present, looked around and said that he had not seen the incident happen.

Please bear in mind that I was still crying – that bodyguard knew what he was doing. Not crying like a baby: just crying like I'd seen a sad movie and didn't want my mates to see me crying.

'Who struck the chef?'

A bodyguard stepped forward. 'I did, President.'

'Why would you do that?'

'I considered the person a threat and took action I thought was necessary.'

'This is our chef. Everyone knows him. Is this your first time here?'

'No, President. I have been with the deputy president for over a year.'

'Then you have seen the chef?'

'Yes, President.'

'Then why did you hit him? He is no threat. He looks after us!'

The president turned to Mary and told her to instruct all the police units that the bodyguard who had struck me was no longer welcome on any government properties. He would have to be dropped off at the gate and await the convoy's return.

'Do you understand that?' the president said to the bodyguard.

The bodyguard left and the deputy president sat down; I closed the door so their meeting could continue.

I walked to the front door to face the bodyguard, but by the time I got there he was walking down to the main gate. I went upstairs, had a quick shower and changed. Needless to say, I had a Noddy nose for a few days.

After that, a lot of the bodyguards whom I didn't know made

an effort to greet me and get to know me. I got permission from Mary to feed all of the bodyguards. After all, we all worked long hours – whatever I could do to improve someone's life, I would do. The only thing I asked in return was that they treated me with the respect that I showed them. I started building a culture at the guesthouse that, on arrival or departure, we would all greet and be polite to one another.

Not everyone seemed to know this, however. On one particular day, the president decided to have a working lunch at the guesthouse. I was notified at about 11 a.m. and started prepping immediately. Approximately an hour later, all the delegates arrived with the president. I ushered them into the lounge for pre-drinks, then went to see Botes and Eddie to inform them that I would make lunch for the staff once the main lunch event had started – the short notice I'd been given affected all of us, and I was sure all the guys would be hungry.

As I was busy serving the main lunch, two traffic police officers walked into the kitchen, demanding food. I asked them which security detail they were on. They informed me that they had led the convoy as the traffic bikes. I asked them to speak to Eddie, as I was going to feed the delegates first.

They became rude and demanding. I walked up to them with my cleaver and told them that my feeding people was a privilege, and not a right – and that if they didn't get out and allow me to continue serving the delegates, I would cut their balls off with my cleaver. I also mentioned that I'd have to be pretty accurate to get their small dingles with my cleaver as well.

I turned to continue plating. Again, they became demanding. I raised my voice and told them to get out of the kitchen immediately. Two of the bodyguards ran into the kitchen. As luck would have it, they were two of the giants on the detail.

'What's the problem, Chef?'

'These two guys are demanding that they eat *now*. I told Eddie I'd feed everyone once I'd served the guests, but they are adamant.'

The two bodyguards walked up to the two speed cops and grabbed them by the collar. They escorted them towards the passage that led to the dining room. I stood there wondering what was happening – the back door was in the opposite direction. Maybe they were going to report them to the security minister.

Then, as they reached the window that looked onto the front entrance, the bodyguards threw them out of it. I could not believe what I had just seen.

Jorrie, one of the bodyguards, stuck his head out the window and, with his loud voice, said, 'Leave our chef alone or you will never eat here again!'

The bodyguards outside all started cheering, then apologised profusely to me. Just before the two giants reached the end of the passage, Jorrie turned to me.

'Chef, it's your rules. We must all be polite.'

Amazed, I gave a weak thumbs-up.

RUMOURS STARTED TO CIRCULATE that the president had found a house in Houghton, Johannesburg, and that he could be moving soon. His residence, one hundred metres up the road in the Libertas estate, was ready – but apparently he wanted to live in Johannesburg. I chose to do the ostrich, sticking my head in the sand and praying that the president would never move out.

I knew the day was coming, but I just kept living in my protected little world. Instead, I decided to do what most men do when we are stressed: we take it out on our wives. I became impossible. I moaned about everything. Nothing was good enough. My wife gave me the best advice – 'Just ask the president!' – but I still found a way to blame her for everything.

I moped around at home, but when anyone else was around I had to be cheerful, a butterfly flitting through a meadow.

During that week, I got a call from the Security Unit one day to inform me that I was to stay at the guesthouse that day and was not allowed to leave. Defiant, I questioned the instruction that had come across more like a command than a request. The only response I got was, 'Just be there, Chef.'

My brain was racing. What had I done or said wrong? It's human nature to think the worst. I went to my office and did paperwork to try to keep busy. This worked, in a way, until I'd catch myself thinking about the call again.

I kept checking the time on the old grandfather clock. Its evil, carved eyes, all hollow and soulless, looking at me, made me doubt myself. Its mouth, all round with its teeth ticking the seconds and minutes away, said, 'Oooh, you're in trouble.'

I stood up and pushed my chair back. I knew I'd done nothing wrong. If there was an issue, I'd sort it out. I'd done nothing wrong.

My phone rang. One of my chefs asked if he could bring two gentlemen to the office – they were looking for me. I asked the chef to keep them there, and told him I was on my way. I knew I was more secure in my kitchen – my happy place, my little haven.

As I walked in and saw the two gentlemen, I thought, *Really? No, seriously – do they all have that mercenary look?* They stood there with their sunglasses on. I did not want to go on a date, so I didn't know why they were trying to look cool. The African gentleman was well-built. You could see the muscles etched under his shirt; his tie was trying to hang on for dear life around his tree-stump neck. His thighs were suffocating in his black pants. The coloured gentleman looked like the good cop. He had a designer beard and cropped hair, and was also tall. If I put on a beat, I swear he would have started rapping to me. (I always do this when I meet people; it's my way of making everyone human, none more important than the other.)

'I presume you are Brett Ladds. We are here from the National Intelligence Agency to meet with you. We require—'

'Hi! How are you, gentlemen? Hope you are having a splendid day! Welcome to the Presidential Guesthouse. I am Brett Ladds – how may I help you?'

The coloured gentleman softened. 'Yes, Chef, you are right. Hi. How are you? I am [name withheld] and this is [name withheld]. We are here to vet you in your position, due to the fact that you deal with the top brass.'

'Pleased to meet you. Would you like something to drink?'

They accepted my offer and I arranged their drinks. I was asked to excuse all the staff from the kitchen, so I sent them on early lunch.

Then, they both picked up fat black briefcases and placed them on my shiny steel kitchen table. They took out files and opened them; with superhuman strength, I strained to see what was in them.

'Firstly, we will be asking you some questions. Are you fine with that?'

'Yes, please do.'

They started with questions about where I had lived and the schools I had been to – general background questions. They made a few statements that were not true, and I corrected them. This made me realise that they could also be trying to catch me out.

'Are you present during the private Sunday meetings that the president holds?'

They knew I was present. On those Sundays, all the security staff would stand outside the guesthouse and protect it, and the other staff would have the day off. I would cater for the meetings – I would walk around, serve drinks and replenish the food for their duration. They would normally run for several hours.

'Yes, I am present. I need to be here to do my duties.'

'What is discussed at these meetings?'

I felt like saying, 'Please can I stick a red-hot poker up my ass? Please?' Instead, I said, 'Sorry, but I will not answer that.'

'You must understand that we have top security clearance. Can you see our badges?'

'Well, if that is the case, then please phone the president and ask him. I'm sure with that clearance you can.'

'Don't get snotty with us. We are here to do our job.'

'Bravo – so am I. I am not politicised. I'm not invited to contribute to the meetings. If you want to know what I serve at them, what's on the menu, I will tell you with pleasure, because that is the scope of my job.'

'This interview is not getting off on the right foot.'

'It would have if you'd asked me the right questions.'

'So, let's do that, then. Have you ever been approached by anyone to inform him or her about what happens in the guesthouse?'

'Yes, I have.'

They scrabbled through their files as if they were cramming for an exam. 'Was this media or political—'

'I don't know. I did not stick around for long enough to find out.'

'What do you mean?'

'When people ask questions like that, I tell them to wait while I call the president's security. Like rabbits down a hole, they disappear.'

'What would make you call a bodyguard?'

'Not just a bodyguard – I would call one of the president's bodyguards, as I know and trust them.'

'So, you're telling me that you hear high-level information being discussed – things that are going to happen, or ways in which situations are being handled politically – and you tell no one?'

'Yes, no one.'

'What about your wife?'

'Seriously, she would kill me if I bored her with information about my job. I do not tell her out of principle; furthermore, she would not care.'

'Would you allow us to hook you up to a lie detector?'

'Sure! I have nothing to hide.'

'Why do the president and his comrades trust you?'

'Please, use your high-level clearance and ask the president. The president asked me to cater for, and serve in, those meetings. I just follow instructions.'

'Tell us, now. At times, there are people who come to see the president after hours. Do you recognise them, or know who they are?'

'Yes, of course I do.'

The two got conniving smiles on their faces. 'Could you name one or two, and tell us what they spoke to the president about?'

'Sure. The man who came on Wednesday loves his coffee sweet with cold milk and enjoys my Parma ham and mustard sandwiches – crust cut off, obviously – and told the president that he really enjoys the way he is treated at the guesthouse and that his wife would kill him if she knew how well he ate when he visited.'

'Do you know this man's name?'

'No. I think he went to the same school as you. He never introduced himself.'

'You're toying with us again.'

'Yes, I am. Please, if this is an issue, do what you have to do – but I am not saying anything.'

'Are you aware that, prior to all the meetings, the room is swept for bugs and explosive devices?'

'Yes, I am. I am the one who requests it to be, through our security.'

'So, if something was leaked, or media found something out, it would have to have come from you.'

'Yes and no. No, as there are other people at those meetings, and yes, as it could be me, but it won't be.'

'So, you would never repeat anything you hear at work – not even for money?'

'Please can we put this to bed? I have never said anything. I will never say anything. Please, polygraph me – you will see. The reason for this is that all I have is my name, Brett Ladds. No money will take that away. Any other questions?'

'Do you know that your dad was politically involved?'

'You must be joking. My dad, no way – he is straight as an arrow.'

As they read from one of the files, they seemed to be looking for evidence to put the last nail in my coffin. 'Your dad's name is Charles Godfrey Ladds?'

'Yes, but you can't hold me accountable for what my dad has or has not done. Please.'

'Yes we can, and we will. It reflects on you and who you are and how you were brought up.'

The file was swung around so I could read it. As I leant forward: 'Do you know that your dad had many dealings with different unions in the country – major unions?'

'Yes, I do. It was part of his job.'

'Do you know that your dad supported black management in the mining industry?'

'Yes, I do. I remember having security around our house and escorting our family on numerous occasions. People on the mine wanted to hurt us.'

'What is a steel shift armband?'

I knew that one – I would go to the mine on Saturdays with my dad to try to impress him, and would speak to my friends' dads, who had to wear them.

'It's a steel plate with leather straps that the African workers had to tie to their upper arms. It had their name, position, area of work and when they started on it.'

'Did you know that your dad had them declared inhuman and illegal on the mines?'

'No, I did not.'

'Did you know that your dad built villages for the mineworkers so their families could live with them, and got rid of the compounds?'

'Yes, of course. I would go play there all the time after school when I lived on the mines. Sorry, but what has this got to do with anything?'

The two stood up. For the first time, they looked human. 'Your dad has been fighting for human rights his whole life. He did more than I think you realise. We have interviewed all your staff and they have great things to say about you. Your background checks out – so we're going to pass you. You must just know that we will check on you periodically, and need to keep your file updated. Any questions?'

'Uh, no. Thank you, I think.'

It was a lot to take in: first I'd been attacked, then made to feel like I'd committed treason, and then my dad, of all people, was made out to be a huge positive in my life.

They took a white envelope from one of the briefcases and started filling out forms. Then came the stamps. They swopped papers, stamped them again, and asked me to sign them.

'I can't just sign them. I need to read them first, please.'

'Your badge is here. I can't just give it to you, though. You need to sign that you received it. It's a National Intelligence Agency badge. We had to give you the rank of captain to allow you access to all areas here, at the Union Buildings, and at other government departments.'

I took one look at the badge, grabbed the pen and signed with pleasure.

I thanked them, and they left; as time went by, we became great friends, and I was pleased to have accumulated more great people in my circle. Whenever we got together, though, you must know that

I had to endure twenty minutes of their laughing about me during that first interview. Then we could move on to having a great time.

I wasn't always perfect, though. I have to amuse you with some stories about this side of me. I know that some of what I did was wrong, and that I did not have the authority to do it, but we all have a little naughtiness in us.

We had just left Witbank after a formal visit to my dad. My wife was adamant that bridges had to be mended and that family was important, so now and then we would go to Witbank to see him. I would put on the false smile and happy persona that I had mastered during my days living at home. What we do for our families ... even then, knowing about the great things he had done on the mines, I still struggled with how we'd been brought up.

It was early on a Sunday morning – I had to get back to the guesthouse for one of the president's private meetings. As I knew the area well, I took a back route onto the highway – a route that had no traffic lights. I had been on the highway for a few minutes when I noticed a police car racing towards me. I moved to the left-hand lane to let it through. In what felt like a split second, the police car was on my tail, flashing its lights. Two police officers gestured to me to pull over. The next thing, they pulled up next to me on the right-hand side, and swerved towards me.

My wife became hysterical, and my kids started crying in the back. I was trying to tell my wife I'd done nothing wrong, but she was adamant that I needed to pull over. We all listen to our wives; I pulled over.

I parked the car in the emergency lane, got out, and made my way to the police car, which had parked in front of me. 'Good morning, officers. Is there a problem?'

A white officer got out, looking like he had missed his coffee that morning. 'You jumped the robot when you left Witbank,' he said in a heavy Afrikaans accent.

'Sorry, officer, I have just driven from 48 Duncan Street. I drove the back route, behind the golf course onto the highway – you know, when you go under the bridge?'

The officer's colleague joined us, pointing at me. 'We saw you. Don't lie to us. You are wasting our time!'

'Not to be disrespectful, but you're wasting *my* time. I did not drive through any traffic lights!'

The two officers went back to their vehicle and returned with a book. The Afrikaans officer said, 'We are going to charge yous for dangerous driving, driving away from the law, and resisting arrest.'

His colleague added, 'I think we just arrest him.'

'Yes, I fink so. Your family will stay here.'

I started to panic. 'Officers, I am not resisting arrest and I am willing to comply. But I did not do what I am charged with doing.'

At the time, I didn't realise it, but I was falling into their trap.

'Okay. You pay us. We pay the fine. Then you get to keep driving. Give me your driver's licence.'

I went to the car to fetch my wallet. My wife, trying to console the kids, was pale as snow. 'What is going on?'

'I think they want a bribe. They say I jumped a traffic light.'

'But you didn't!'

'I know, my girl. But please, one argument at a time.'

'Don't pay them! We are not those people, do you hear me?'

I walked back to the police officers and opened my wallet to take out my driver's licence.

'Look there, lots of pink notes, hey?' the Afrikaans officer ventured.

His colleague smiled as if his slot machine had just hit the jackpot. I handed my licence to the officer. And just then, it was as if the sun had risen after a long, dark night in the woods: there before me was my National Intelligence Agency badge, rank and all. 'Sorry, officers, here is my other licence.' I held the badge out to them. 'May I quickly get your names, as I would like to phone this in?'

'Flash a-ah!' the song rolled in my head. The fastest man in the universe could have learnt a lesson from these two. They threw my cards into my face, jumped into the car, did a U-turn on the highway straight through the shrubs on the median, and were gone.

I picked up my badge and licence, and went back to my car. I got in, put my seatbelt on and started driving. I heard nothing but the tyres on the road as we sat in silence for a while.

'What just happened, Brett?'

I told my wife and she sat back in her seat. 'They won't come after us again, will they?'

'No, I think we've seen the last of them.'

I told the story at a braai we had a week later. As entertaining as it was then, it was scary when it happened.

The score was 1–0 to me: I'd used my badge for justice, so I'd done good with it.

A long weekend soon came up, with the public holiday on a Monday. I invited all my friends to go down to the coast with us. Excited, we got into our cars and off to Margate we went – a real youngster party place on the south coast of KwaZulu-Natal.

On the Saturday night, we went to a beach party and danced the night away. We really had a great time. I stopped drinking a few hours before we planned to leave, as I did not want to drink and drive. After a few litres of water and some energy drinks, I was fine. We all met at our cars to drive back to our holiday house, which was ten minutes away.

We drove off in convoy. By the time I reached the outskirts of Margate, I was enjoying the corners a little too much. As I came around one of them, I saw a roadblock.

A police officer indicated to me to pull over. As I stopped, I jumped out of my car – I did not want the officer to see my friend passed out on the back seat.

'Evening, sir. Have you been drinking tonight?'

'Yes, officer. I stopped just after 9 p.m. and have been drinking water ever since.'

'That's very responsible of you. Well done.'

'Thank you, officer.' I felt like my teacher had just given me a gold star.

'It's a pity I'm stopping you for speeding, though. You were doing sixty kilometres an hour over the speed limit. That means I need to arrest you.'

'Dammit, man.'

'Sir, did you say something?'

'No, officer. Sorry. Just speaking to myself in disgust.'

The officer waved and a junior came running up. 'Place this man under arrest and put him in the van.'

'Yes, sir,' said the junior as he handcuffed me.

The senior officer turned back to me. I took the chance: 'Sorry, officer. Please may I ask you a favour? May I beg you to help me? You seem to be a reasonable man. I know I'm at fault, but I just don't want to lose my job.'

'Yes, young man. How can I help?'

Handcuffed, I asked the officer to take my wallet out. I told him that in my wallet was a business card, and asked him if he could phone my boss and explain that I would not be at work on Tuesday. The officer opened my wallet, willing to assist me.

'Young man, why have you got an NIA badge in here?'

'Officer, I use it for my job. Please take out the business card behind it and phone my boss?'

He did not look amused with me now – I think he felt I was taking a chance. He was correct: I was praying that what he would see on the business card would get me out of this pickle.

He removed the card, a white rectangle with the country's coat of arms embossed on it in gold and the president's name and a number on it.

'Are you jerking me around?'

'No, officer. I work for the president.'

Then, the officer did something I could never have expected: he took out his phone and dialled the number. I felt my insides running out of my bottom. With each digit he dialled, he looked at me.

'Hello, this is Officer [name withheld] from the KZN police department. Who am I speaking to?'

I heard a faint voice on the other side, and the officer nodded. There was a brief conversation, and then he said, 'Will do,' and hung up.

He stood there for a while; his phone rang again. 'Yes sir, yes, I will do so, thank you sir, yes sir, it will happen immediately.'

The senior officer placed all my cards back into my wallet and pushed it back into my pants. He walked behind me and took the handcuffs off. 'Young man, I don't know who you are, but one thing is for sure – you are going to get more shit from your boss Mary than I could ever get you into, and for the commissioner to have phoned me to release you, you must really be someone. I'm glad I'm not you. There is another roadblock down the road. Drive carefully.'

Just like that, he turned and walked away.

I returned to my car, my friend still passed out, my other friends driving away. As I drove back to the holiday house like Miss Daisy's driver, I wished I *had* been arrested. I spent the rest of the weekend in panic.

When I returned to work on Tuesday, I slunk around waiting for a hiding. At about lunchtime, Mary's car stopped outside and she came running up the stairs. I was busy with a fruit basket; she grabbed a handful of grapes.

'*Yhu wena*, you're lucky the meeting went on late and I got the phone. Next time *loshia wena* (I'm going to beat you).'

'Sorry, Mary.'

'You young boys are all the same.'

She got back into her car and drove off.

That was it – not even worth worrying about. I believe she knew, though, that what I had put myself through had been punishment enough.

The score? 1–1. I chose to keep it that way, and behaved.

THE FOLLOWING WEEK was the Cabinet's annual braai at the Union Buildings, hosted by President Mandela. My wife and I had been invited; that night, I was to be a guest. As we arrived, everybody greeted me. It was amazing that all the ministers knew my name, and that I was greeted as an equal.

I stood some distance away and looked at all these great men and women, a glass of wine in my hand, watching the president laugh and enjoy his comrades and their company. My wife was chatting to some of the ministers and having a great time, which she deserved. One of the ministers had taken a liking to her; I could tell this complimented her.

I turned back to look at the president and it struck me that all the great times, the experiences and his wonderful advice were coming to an end. My guilt about how I had treated my wife, and my heart, breaking with the knowledge that I would no longer be seeing see the president every day, weighed so heavily that I could not take it any longer.

I went inside and sat on the stairs, my eyes flooded and a tear in my chest I could not mend. The person who loved me the most I'd been treating like crap, all because I'd been too much of a coward to confront the truth about the president's departure. I wanted to run, but didn't know where.

'Chef, what are you doing? This is a happy occasion.'

I jumped up, trying to wipe my tears away. This only caused my eyes to burn more.

'Sorry, President. I am just having a bad day.'

The president sat on the stair next to me and asked me again what was wrong. You couldn't lie to this president – he would see right through you.

I told him how badly I had treated my wife, and why. I was expecting a lecture; instead, he gave me the greatest advice for how to make things right with her. After a while, I was happy and positive again, and just wanted to hug my wife and never let her go. As he stood up, he looked at me: 'Now, take my advice. I am the president, you know.'

I sprung to my feet. If I did not have so much respect for the president, I would have hugged him. As he started heading back to the braai, he turned again and looked at me. 'The other matter we will discuss tomorrow. Tonight is casual. No work.'

I went to the bathroom and tried to fix myself up as best I could. Then I went straight to the bar and had a still Glenfiddich, Spiderman style – you know, from the index finger to the pinky. I stood back and watched my beautiful wife. After several minutes, she looked up and saw me appreciating all of her. She walked over to me and hugged me and I was forgiven.

She just knew.

Years later, I told her about the advice I had got and from whom. She looked disappointed. I asked why; she said that if she had known it was that easy, she would have asked the president to intervene more often when he came around to our flat.

The next day, hungover as hell, I went to fetch the president for breakfast. I tried to behave like nothing was wrong. We walked down to the Breakfast Room. As we walked that familiar passageway, I thanked the president for the invitation and told him what an honour it had been to be there.

He sat down, and I went to fetch his breakfast. When I returned, he asked me to sit with him.

'I am leaving the guesthouse. But I would like to ask you, would you please stay on and host all the delegates that visit our country, as well as my friends whom I would like to invite? Before you answer, I will still be coming often for breakfast and lunches, as the Union Buildings are just down the road.'

I stood up, not quite thinking clearly, as you will read next: I saluted the president. Today, I often think how stupid I was. The president must surely have told all his friends and had a laugh at my expense – which I deserved.

'Yes please, President. Yes please,' I said.

'Well, then, it's decided. Mary will come and chat to you. She will sort the rest out.'

I turned, ready to run upstairs to tell my wife before she left for work. But as I got to the door: 'Chef, you see, as I told you last night, life seems to work things out for us.'

I was about to burst into tears, so I decided to do a bow and leave as quickly as possible. Crying twice in front of the president? *Really*.

The president moved out a few days later. With his advice at my back and his confidence in me as my suit of armour, I was ready to host dignitaries from the world's highest echelons.

But was I, really?

With over twenty state visits from presidents and vice presidents from around the world, royalty from the world's oldest royal houses, and the most famous celebrities still to cross my path, the adventure that was my life was not even halfway.

7
A rough ride

I GOT OVER MYSELF, EVENTUALLY – and we started to change the guesthouse into a seven-star establishment.

Being a government department, we had to follow the rules and regulations of every other department we worked with. This was an experience – one that could be a comedy show all on its own.

Christian had stepped back, as he'd planned to do. He was ready to pick up on all that longed-for spare time. He was happy that he had been part of the historic inauguration; I realised that, after all the long hours he would have worked every day at the Diplomatic Guesthouse, he was ready to rest. I knew, though, that having his continued full-time involvement would have made things a lot easier, given all his contacts and influence – the work we were setting out to do would have been as smooth as Michael Jackson moonwalking across the stage.

The first things that needed attention were the curtains and carpets throughout the house. Many guests who came to the guesthouse were in awe of the decor initially, and could not stop complimenting how the rooms were dressed. I, too, was that naive in the beginning, which I put down to two things. One: being starstruck ('I am really here!'). Two: having no taste. It was obvious that the guesthouse had been dressed to cater for the taste of the old regime. The main thing for us was to ensure that the guesthouse was world-class. To add to the pressure, Queen Elizabeth II had accepted the president's invitation to visit South Africa.

Getting the government's Public Works department to start painting the guesthouse was quite easy. As the guesthouse is a heritage site, we did not want to change the colours drastically. We got all the exterior walls painted white. The handmade shutters had been painted green. Originally, we tried to get them stripped to their natural wood finish, but we lost that one. We were adamant, though, that all the old wooden doors (most of which were handmade) be stripped of paint, refurbished, and only a natural varnish be applied to protect the wood. Every door and window that was removed to be painted needed its brass fittings taken off and polished to a mirror finish. We retained the white interior walls, adding a beige tint to some of the walls to break the look.

The house was like a bride choosing a dress for her wedding. It had to be perfect.

We chose light, sand-coloured carpets for the entire house to ensure uniformity. They were made of thick wool – I just could not wait for them to be installed so that, when everyone had gone home that night, I could roll around on them.

While the painting was happening, we decided that we were going to start fixing up the suites one at a time. We started in the main suite, Suite 1 (really, ten out of ten for that name; I suppose some brainpower was exhausted after putting it together). Once the room had been painted, we had the carpets installed. The white tiles in the bathroom were not bad at all, so we just had new grouting done between them.

Then, there was the issue of the pink toilet. You would not believe it, but the toilet in the main suite was pink. We contacted one of the directors at the Public Works department and set up a meeting – just an informal one, to show him how far we had come and to discuss a few more issues that needed to be resolved. Bear in mind that the ANC was still in the process of filtering its own people into all the departments, and had only got to top management by this stage. The reason for this was that the president had informed everyone that all rules and procedures would be followed in all areas of staffing.

So, this director arrived and walked around, looking pleased with himself, almost as if he had painted the guesthouse himself. He had a huge, red nose, like a cartoon character with a bottle sticking out of his back pocket and bubbles floating out of his head from drinking. His cheap cologne could not disguise the smell of the discount liquor he must have drunk the previous night; the only creases his clothes had were around his big butt, where the seat he sat on all day at work had made its imprint. As we walked around, he was friendly to his colleagues yet rude and abrupt to us, as if we were his enemy.

We wanted to take him to Suite 1 to show him some issues we had, and to ask whether he could help with them. As we started to climb the stairs to the suites, we heard the director gasping for breath like a goldfish that had managed to jump out of its bowl: 'Is there not any chance of just telling me what is the problem?'

I turned around politely: 'No, sir. Please, we need you to come and see for yourself.'

Really, only one floor up and this pile of lard was almost convulsing. It reminded me of one of my friends who thought he could dance, once – when he tried, I could hear ambulances rushing to the club to save him from a seizure on the dance floor.

Eventually we reached Suite 1. He looked around. 'Ja, everyfing is good.'

So far, perhaps. 'sir, please could you come and look in the bathroom?' I said.

'What is the problem?'

'Look, sir, I would like to thank you for all your effort to date, but the toilet is screaming pink.'

'How can a toilet scream?'

Oh my soul, I was boiling inside. This bubble-butt had so much authority, and I had to kiss so much ass to have anything done. It was sickening: my lips could spend a year kissing his ass without kissing the same place twice. 'Sorry, sir. I was just trying to point out the elephant in the room, to use an expression.'

'Very, very funny. You fink you are *slim* (clever).'

'But do you see the problem, sir?'

'No, I fink it's fine. A *kakhuis* is a *kakhuis*. All you do is crap in it.'

'I agree, sir, but we're going to have the most important people in the world coming to the guesthouse. We want to show our country at its best. Surely we can change the toilet to a white one? All our linen and towels are bright white. Please can we change the toilet?'

'No. You are eating my budget wif dis place.'

'Please, sir. I beg you.'

'No.'

That was that: we had already spent thousands on the suite, but couldn't spend a couple of hundred rands on a toilet.

'Which way is the *hysbak* (lift)?'

As he asked me, I had an idea. I distracted him by pointing out a few blemishes on the wall that had just been painted; as he went to inspect, I ran to the distribution board on the far end of the passage and switched off the circuit breaker for the lift. By the time I got back to the door of the suite, he had already instructed his painters to fix the wall.

'This way, sir.'

We reached the lift and he pushed the button. Nothing happened, I could see his whole world fall apart as he contemplated making the trip downstairs. I smiled at him, laughing to myself.

'See you downstairs, sir.'

I ran downstairs and phoned Mary to intervene, but got a '*Suka wena!* (Go away!)' from her. She told me to sort it out myself.

Later that same day, I had a call from the British High Commissioner asking for a quick site inspection. He had to report back to London in preparation for Her Highness's state visit. I welcomed the inspection and scheduled it for the following morning. This was my opportunity to remove the pink toilet. I knew that lardass director was just being difficult as the ANC was in power. I was going to have to use all my diplomatic 'skills'.

The following morning, a few of the High Commission officials arrived. As I showed them around, I could see they were impressed. I then took them up to Suite 1, where Queen Elizabeth would be staying. All the furniture was still wrapped as it stood on the woolly carpet, the white walls crisp and clean. The linen and towels in the cupboards had been washed and wrapped. We were almost there.

So, I invited them to inspect the bathroom.

'Oh my goodness – what is *that*?' asked one of the officials.

'It's a glow-in-the-dark toilet, so our guests can find it in the dark,' I said.

She gave me a blank look.

'Really, my lady, I am just joking.'

'Well, let me inform you that the toilet *will* be changed. It is not acceptable.'

'Your wish is my command. Please may I ask you to mail the South African desk with all the changes you want? I will ensure that they happen.'

'Everything we have seen is perfect. Just get rid of that loo!'

We completed the inspection. I walked them to their car, opening the women's doors for them. Once they'd got in, I popped my head into the car.

'Please don't forget the mail about the toilet? And, if I may ask, please flag it as important?'

'Will do,' they said, and off they drove.

My phone rang just after lunch. 'What did you do? You think you are funny? What is this about?'

'Hi, Mary. How are you, Madam?'

'Stop being charming! What is this?'

'I don't know what you are talking about?'

'I know you. This was you.'

'Madam, you told me to handle it, so I did. That fat man was not going to do it and I did not want to bother the minister.'

'So you made it my problem?'

The phone went dead.

All this to change a pink toilet. *Really.*

My phone rang again. Expecting another earful, I answered, 'Hello my mama Mary.'

'Who are you calling your mama?'

'Hello, Director. Sorry, I thought you were someone else.'

'You fink you're funny? My boss *kakked* in my ear. Now I *have* to change that *kak* toilet. You fink you're special? Never phone me again. I want a bottle of brandy for this, too.'

'No, sir, you will not be getting anything from me. I asked for your assistance and you refused. So please, sir, do your job. If you don't assist in future, I will do this again. Have a stunning day, sir.'

I put the phone down with a sense of great achievement.

Just as I'd battled to be accepted by the ANC family, I could see that another fight was brewing – that the old civil service had not yet accepted the new regime, and that everything was going to be a problem. The pink toilet got me thinking about how to handle people who displayed a similar attitude. After that day, any work that the Public Works department did at the guesthouse was done with animosity. I knew the lardass had got to everyone in his department.

I would feed all the workers every day to thank them, but after the toilet incident only the black workers would eat with us. The whiteys refused. So sad.

We had ordered the most beautiful crockery and cutlery, all imported, for the guesthouse's state banquets – gold-rimmed plates (not kitsch at all, just a simple gold band on the rim of each plate), and heavy silver cutlery that shone like diamonds on a jeweller's workbench. It was nothing short of perfection.

In the passage opposite the scullery was an old safe. It took almost two of me to open the door. Once again, we contacted Director Lardass and asked to have shelves installed in the safe: we wanted to lock the crockery and cutlery away, for obvious reasons. For him, I think, not so obvious.

The next day, the carpenters arrived with tools and wood. I was in the scullery, assisting the staff to wash and count all the crockery and cutlery. I showed them to the safe, then returned to my work. A little later, excited to see everything falling into place, I went to see how far the workers had got with the shelves. The first few shelves had been put up. But something wasn't right.

'Sorry, sir. Don't you think the shelves are a bit flimsy for the weight of all the stock? It's very heavy.'

'*Fokkof* (Fuck off),' he said.

'I don't mean to be rude, but I do understand Afrikaans. That was not nice.'

'Listen, *Engelsman* (Englishman). I know my job. I've been doing it for a long time. If you think you and your kind are going to come and take my job away, you can think again.'

'Sir, we all work for the same government. I don't want your job. I just do woodwork as a hobby.'

'You said you understand Afrikaans?'

'I do, Sir. Why?'

'Then listen: *fokkof*.'

So I did. I went back to cleaning and counting everything. He was not going to dampen my excitement. I continued laughing and joking with the staff.

At the end of the day, my fellow government employee stuck his head into the scullery.

'*Alles is reg* (Everything is done).'

This man had really offended me. I knew it was not Afrikaans culture to do so – Botes and his unit were Afrikaans, yet they were amazing. Eddie Meiring, and a lot of his team, were Afrikaans, and they were the most beautiful, kind, caring and positive men. I put it down to the department and its management. All the English, Afrikaans, Indian and black people I worked with were a family, all enjoying deepening our friendship pool.

Nevertheless, we tugged a little on the shelves and they seemed fine. So, we loaded all the beautiful cutlery and crockery onto them. I locked up and went upstairs for the night.

Deep in the night, a truck just missed a turn, crashed into parked cars and rolled as it ploughed into the surrounding shops. Seconds before the truck was going to hit me, I woke from my horrific dream and sat up in bed. Beads of sweat trickled down my brow.

My son started crying; my wife leapt out of bed.

'Did you hear that, Brett?'

'I thought it was a dream!'

'No no no, that was here, even the floor shook.'

I told her to go to comfort our son. As I walked down the passage in my Superman shorts and wife-beater vest, I radioed the control room for immediate assistance.

Know one thing: I would die for my family, but if you need a hero, don't look at my Superman shorts – look at my sneakers. They were meant for running, and that's exactly what they would do.

In no time, the police were at the guesthouse, the control room being only twenty-five metres away. Flashlights strobed all over the house. As we searched the building, with the police switching lights on as we went, we saw nothing unusual.

A few minutes later, the dog unit arrived. One of the policemen turned to me and asked whether I'd noticed how pretty the police officer was who ran the unit – blonde, finely built, sky-blue eyes. She *was* pretty, so I said yes, but reminded him that I was married and that my wife was upstairs.

'Chef, I am not insinuating anything. But for your wife's sake, the dog handlers' sake and, most of all, your own, I would go put some underpants on. I'm sure that's not a baton you've got hanging out the side there.'

I gave him a grin, followed by a tap on the back, and immediately turned around to run upstairs to go do as I'd been so politely advised to do.

As I turned towards the kitchen passage, then right at the scullery, I passed the safe.

'Fuuuuuck.'

The realisation hit me: the crash could have been all that gorgeous new crockery and cutlery in the safe. I ran. I fetched my keys, and put underpants on. Baton in its holster, I went back downstairs. It felt as if someone had just put my brain in a liquidiser.

I called the police officer to assist me, and we opened the safe door. Before me lay the most beautiful shards of crockery, the ears that were once teacup handles lying helplessly, trying to hear whether there had been any survivors. The scratched cutlery in the rubble of the crockery looked as if it had been digging all night to uncover the signs of life the ears had heard.

The police officer looked at me, his eyes as big as the sideplates used to be.

'*Now* you're in *kak*.'

'Thanks, bud. I can see that for myself.'

He radioed everyone to tell them that the situation was under control; I asked him to help me to lock up and turn the lights back off. As he walked out, he turned to fist-bump me.

'Good luck, Chef,' he said, then vanished into the night.

I went upstairs and got back into bed. All I could do was hope that the truck would jump out of my dreams and hit me, as it had intended.

I walked the long way around the kitchen, to avoid the scene of the crime. To be honest, I did not even want to *see* the safe. I waited until 8:15 a.m., then phoned the director. No answer.

I phoned a few more times. Nothing.

I then sent Amos, our waiter-cum-driver, to deliver a message to him on paper: *Your guys screwed up. Everything was destroyed when your shelves collapsed.* It took Amos thirty minutes to get there. Fifty-five minutes after Amos left, Lardass arrived. The way he jumped out of the car and dashed up the stairs convinced me that the struggles of the other day had been just an act.

I opened the safe door with assistance. There the director stood. Then, he turned around with a hundred and one questions, asked so sweetly that I thought he was hitting on me.

'Okay, leave this to me,' he said, before walking out.

I contacted Mary. She advised me to take Lardass's advice and leave it to him. Needless to say, everything we requested to be done at the guesthouse from that moment was done – with perfection. In record time. We even got proper shelving in the safe. Days later, the shelves were as full as they had been before the disaster. To this day, I cannot explain who paid, what happened to the broken stock, and how the new stock arrived as quickly as it did.

Life went on.

The whole guesthouse was beautiful, fit for all the world's kings, queens and presidents. I did practice runs with the team so that all the staff knew what was where, what was expected of everyone, and how to work as a team. While they were busy perfecting their routines, I started putting my order together for what the first few state banquets required. I then made an appointment at Foreign Affairs so the orders could be placed, following the correct channels.

I took my paperwork and went to the admin office. I even took a platter of snacks – I knew I would be there a while, and was hoping I could butter them up so things could run more smoothly.

I walked into the office for the first time and introduced myself.

'A great day to you all. I am Brett Ladds, the chef at the Presidential Guesthouse.'

On my left was a thin, funny-looking man with a big head. His hair was a winner: it had a huge wave in front that sloped away towards the back of his head. He looked like a golf ball on a tee with a ginormous fringe. I could see that, when he was young, he used to dress like Roy Orbison. A woman must have told him the look suited him, as he still wore the glasses. His brilliant white legs ended in long, narrow feet in well-worn shoes.

Come on, I thought to myself. *Do cartoonists get their characters from government departments? Must there always be a fat one, a thin one and a weird-looking woman?* The other guy was a bit thickset, with a neat, shaven head as if he was in the military. He had these cheeks you just wanted to pinch. And he had a soul patch. A soul patch is the little tuft of hair that men grow under their bottom lip when they cannot grow a beard.

'Where may I sit, please?'

The daggers in their eyes stabbed the open chair next to Golf Ball on a Tee. I sat.

'Please could you assist me with the orders for the guesthouse? I've had all suppliers fill in the forms to become vendors for the department.'

As I handed over the forms, Golf Ball took them, then stood up and dropped them on Soul Patch's desk.

'Would you like some of the snacks I made?'

They stood up, taking their cups off their saucers. They piled their saucers high, saying, 'Don't think you can bribe us!' as they did so.

'I don't! I just thought that, since we were going to be here for a while as this is my first time, we could at least enjoy it.'

'Good. But don't bribe us.'

I got that the first time, I thought.

'Last time we were given a list and told to buy what was on it. This time we do things properly, understand?'

'I do. Sorry about that. It was not my intention.'

They started putting the items on my lists, and their prices, onto the system. Once they had finished, they printed out their list and sat down. Each took a ruler and started crossing some items off. They highlighted other items.

I sat there for an hour watching my Beavis and Butthead do their thing. It was like pulling teeth.

Then, 'Okay, Brett Chef, this is what you can order and where you can order from.'

That's when I made a gigantic mistake. I laughed. Not just a hahaha, either – I laughed from my core. What they had told me, multiplied by the way they looked, plus the way they worked – I just couldn't hold it in any longer.

After wiping away my tears, I asked if they were serious.

'Excuse us, but we have been here for over ten years each. We know our jobs. How did we entertain you?'

'Forgive me – it's just that you can't choose what I can and can't buy. All the items on that list are required.'

As Soul Patch stood up, he sighed and walked over. He leant over me with his pen, attacking the printout.

'You can't buy peanut oil, olive oil or balsamic vinegar. You must use sunflower oil and spirit vinegar. We have a contract with a company that supplies these. The meat is far too expensive. Why must you get veal from Holland and rib-eye steak that is R60 more than the brisket? I crossed those out and increased the brisket.'

'Sir, please, please allow me to explain. The president has invited his guests from around the world. We need to host them in the way to which they are accustomed. Look at the stock I purchased while the president was staying at the guesthouse—'

'We have no idea what you purchased then. All those expenses went through the Presidency, not Foreign Affairs.'

I tried approaching it from a different angle. 'Sirs, please let me explain what I would normally serve during a state banquet. In the morning, I make cold-meat platters—'

Golf Ball on a Tee cut in: 'Parma ham for R1426 a kilogram? Are you crazy? Just last week my wife and I bought ninety-seven grams of sandwich ham for R77 a kilogram. I had it on my sandwich today and it was delicious.'

'Please, sir, let's compare apples with apples. Parma ham is a twenty-year-old ham matured in the Alps. If I served sandwich ham, I would be jobless faster than your sandwich would hit the floor after leaving a dignitary's hand.'

I realised that we were playing a game of tennis, and that these two morons had brought their wives' knitting needles to use as racquets. I have no problem with educating people or tying to help them see things. But when people don't know and are arrogant at the same time, the rocket inside me explodes.

'Sirs, please just let me say that being born stupid is most acceptable, but dying stupid is extremely sad. I will be taking this matter elsewhere. I am tired of the roadblocks I reach just to do my job. Gentlemen: good day. I hope I never see you again.'

I stood up and walked out, then went back to fetch my platter.

I went to fetch my wife at work and my son from school. I could not stop moaning to my wife about what had just happened. As we drove past the Union Buildings towards Bryntirion Estate, there in front of us was one of the deputy ministers, Aziz Pahad, walking along the road. I pulled over.

'Afternoon, Minister. Why are you walking?'

'Chef, I'm just taking a brisk walk home for some lunchtime exercise, then I have a meeting in fifty minutes.'

'Minister, let me give you a lift? It's another three kilometres.

In that suit, you will be hot and bothered, and you'll never make it back in time for your meeting.'

'I didn't realise it was so far! It always goes so quickly when I am driven.'

He jumped into the car.

Then, my wife had to go and say, 'Tell the minister! The minister will help. Surely he understands.'

Oh crap. What had she just done?

'Yes, tell me, Chef. How can I help?'

My wife flashed me her go-on-you-had-the-balls-just-now-to-rant-and-rave-where-are-they-now look.

'Minister, do you want the funny version or the serious one?'

I told him the whole story and begged him not to get anyone into trouble – just to put it down to ignorance. When I dropped him off, he reassured me that he would be diplomatic and that I didn't need to worry. Everything would be sorted out.

I received my stock that week. From then on, I only sent lists to Foreign Affairs.

It had been a rough ride.
> *Guesthouse revamped: thanks, Director Lardass.*
> *Decor ready: thanks, amazing Judy Michel.*
> *Kitchen and bar stocked: thanks, eventually, to Golf Ball on a Tee and Soul Patch.*
> *Security perfect: thanks, Eddie and Botes.*

But now, the guesthouse was perfect.

8
Receiving royalty

It was March 1995, and Queen Elizabeth was coming to visit President Mandela. The guesthouse may have been perfect, but there was so much else involved in preparing for a state visit. So, first, let me give you a quick rundown – I don't want to go into too much detail, otherwise I'd have to call this book *How to Prepare for a State Visit.*

It all started at the Department of Foreign Affairs: 'Hello! Want to come visit us? We have the coolest president, a beautiful country, some impressive mountains and a rich culture.' No kidding: all political relations with other countries ran through what was then the Department of Foreign Affairs. The department had different desks, such as the Asian desk. These desks would handle the visits, depending on which country was involved.

The department would contact the Presidency about the visit. Once dates had been confirmed, the Protocol office, under the legendary John Reinders at the time, would get involved. Foreign Affairs would then receive an agenda from the visiting country and send its own agenda to that country in turn. This would go back and forth until the state visit itself.

Then, the meetings would start. These took place at the guesthouse. Here is a list of the different organisations and departments that would attend the meetings:

Department of Foreign Affairs
The Presidency

The police
The bodyguard unit
Me, representing the Presidential Guesthouse
Representatives from the embassy of the visiting country
Representatives from the government of the visiting head of state

Quite a few meetings were required to arrange the following:
The head of state's arrival and departure
Key people involved in the visit
Where the head of state would be staying
The guests' dietary requirements
The meetings to be scheduled during the visit
Agendas for these meetings
The state banquet, including the guest list and speeches
A list of people involved and their authorisation levels
Security for the visiting head of state
Security while in convoy
Security at all the places to which the visiting head of state would travel
Security at the guesthouse
Places of interest to visit, and so on.

The result of all the meetings would be comprehensive planning of requirements, places, people involved, contact details, security plans and a to-the-minute schedule. All the different departments and people involved would work from this as their instruction and their mandate.

I was hosting such a meeting for a state visit once when my mother popped into the lounge area, where the meeting was taking place. Needless to say, everyone's attention was drawn to this woman who had just arrived: they all looked at her, waiting for her to introduce herself, apologise for being late and take her seat. When I saw her, my head dropped. I wanted to dissolve right there in my chair, like a headache tablet.

'Hello everyone! I am Anne Ladds. How are you?'

They all just bobbed their heads, like those nodding dogs in the back windows of cars.

Then, 'Hello, my son!'

I froze and gave my mom a death stare, hoping that some superpower would enter my body and the rays from my eyes would send her into another dimension. Then, I defrosted, stood up, walked straight over to her, and gently put my arm around her to escort her out of the meeting. But, like dog poo that you walk onto your carpet, she stuck there.

'Hello my sweetheart. How are you?'

Like a fish, she slipped out of my hold and walked closer to the attendees. 'You must just tell me if Brettie doesn't behave himself.'

Under my breath, I fumed, 'Please can we go speak outside?'

'*Ciao ciao!*' she said, as she waved her way out.

I happened to be chairing that state visit meeting; present were an ambassador, the directors of different departments, representatives from Special Forces and the police, and bodyguards, all of whom I could hear having a good snigger at my expense as I steered my mom down the passage.

When we got to the kitchen, I asked her what was so important.

'Oh, I just popped in to say hi.'

'How did you get in here – and how did you even get onto the estate?'

'I just told them who I was, and that you were my son, and if they did not let me in I would ask you to deal with them.'

'Mom, you need to be placed on a visitors' list to be allowed in here – and you can't use my name like that!'

She just smiled and said, 'Well, I'm here now. Can we have some tea?'

'No! I'm in a meeting – you know, the one you just embarrassed me in?'

'Okay, well, if that's your attitude I won't pop in again.'

I stormed back to the meeting, offering more tea and coffee as I walked in while dying inside. Of course, every time we had a meeting after that, the joke was on me.

THERE WERE HUNDREDS OF PEOPLE running around the guesthouse the day the Queen was due to arrive. Except in the service area, where all the kitchens and working areas were – this was out of bounds for everyone but me and my team. We were ready, and did not want any security issues.

Later that day, my wife got home from work and went to take her usual seat at the window, from which where she would watch the guests arrive. I had all those who were not mentioned in our ops meeting book leave the guesthouse. I then got our police unit at the front door to do a sweep. After their sweep, the dog unit arrived, and searched the whole house to ensure everything was safe. Police were placed at every exit, and only our police unit was allowed in the guesthouse once the final sweeps had been done.

I sent the team to freshen up. I ran upstairs to do the same and change my suit. Standing in front of mirror perfecting my suit – ensuring that each cuff was straight, my tie and suit jacket met each other at a perfect angle, and my laces were identically tied, I heard the radio.

'Ten minutes out. Main gate, are you ready?'

'Yes, Captain. We are in format and standing ready.'

'Guesthouse, are you ready?'

'Yes, Captain. Just waiting for the Chef to come to the front door.'

'Chef, are you there?'

'Yes, I am on my way down.'

All the staff were lined up in the passage. I did this for each visit to allow our guests to familiarise themselves with my team, as this would be their home for the next few days.

I stood at the door, loud and proud: I was representing South Africa, and was going to be working with the Queen. Think about that: millions of people go to the UK just to see the palace where the Queen resides, and tens of thousands of people line the streets to get a glimpse of her as her convoy drives past.

The radio channel went quiet.

We were all on guard when the radio silence broke: 'Abort, abort, abort. Suspect seen in the window.'

I spun around faster than a Frisbee gliding downwind. Our security unit turned and took a stance, ready to attack the threat. All hearts pounded together, like the drums of Zulu warriors after defeating their enemy on the battlefield.

As my eyes saw the threat, I grabbed my radio.

'No reason to abort. It's my wife.'

I looked at the bodyguard who had called it in and wanted to hit him with a slippery, wet fish. I got so flustered that my neck started burning and my palms started sweating. All the bodyguards knew my wife. We lived there – she walked around the guesthouse freely. Before I could make my next move, I saw the convoy gliding up.

Great. There I stood like an overripe tomato with nice sweaty palms. The perfect way to greet the Queen of England.

I lifted up my suit jacket and wiped my hands on my cotton shirt. Then I tried to slow my breathing to calm myself down.

The leader jumped out of the front convoy car, then the Queen's bodyguards jumped out of the Queen's car. Time froze as they looked around; then their eyes locked and, at a slight tilt of their heads, all the security jumped out of all the vehicles.

The car door on the far side opened and Prince Philip got out. He walked around the car. As he reached the Queen's door, one of her bodyguards opened it and the Queen exited the car. Before me stood the Queen of England and Prince Philip. I started to welcome them with half a bow: 'Welcome to South Africa, and welcome to the Presidential Guesthouse of South Africa. I am Brett Ladds, the executive chef and manager, and I am here to serve you during your stay, Your Majesty and Prince.' How I got all that right was amazing.

'Thank you so much, Brett. We look forward to our stay,' Prince Philip said.

I then turned and, with a gentle gesture, said, 'Please follow me.'

The Queen's bodyguard bolted in front of me. He had eyes like a chameleon, inspecting everything at once.

We walked up the stairs. I had no idea what to do or say, so I did the next best thing: I just walked. As we got to the top of the stairs, I saw the staff. Yes! I could break the awkward silence!

'Your Majesty and Prince, please meet my team.'

As we walked past each person, I said his or her name. He or she would step forward for the Queen and Prince's greeting.

We started to walk up the next flight of stairs towards the suites. The Queen asked if they could have some tea in their room while they freshened up.

Wow! The Queen had just spoken to me!

'That would be my pleasure, Your Majesty.'

I could hear one of my maître d's turn and walk down the stairs as he heard the request. We already knew all our guests' likes and dislikes, food and drink requests, and spoils. So, we knew how to serve this royal couple with perfection.

I stopped at Suite 1. 'Please could you enter your suite?' I said with a courteous bow.

'Thank you.'

Wow. The Queen had spoken to me *again*. I know I keep going on about this, but when you first engage with a president, royalty or celebrity your heart naturally skips a few beats. I walked through the suite and explained all the facilities. The room was brilliant white, with the African sunlight filling the room with all its splendour. We had brushed the fibres of the carpet in the same direction throughout the suite.

Flowers had been placed strategically in the rooms. Even they were at attention, showing their colours in the hope that the Queen would lean towards them to experience their beautiful aromas. The two fruit bowls showed the diversity of our great nation through the variety of their fruits. The drinks cabinet glasses beamed their light in sparkles around the room, as if no fingerprint had ever tarnished their radiance.

I could sense the Queen's approval.

'Thank you. This is most beautiful,' she said.

I then showed her how to contact me or her security, and how to dial an outside line.

'Chef, tea for Suite 1.'

'Thank you once again. I look forward to our stay here.'

Walking out of Suite 1, I felt proud of how I had handled myself. My dealings with President Mandela had taught me that we all are human, and all deserve equal respect.

I made my way down to the main lounge, where all the delegates were enjoying refreshments and light snack platters. I walked over to the Queen's bodyguard, who had already placed his security on the top floor, and introduced myself. I asked him to come and meet guesthouse security in the house. Having brought them together, I left them to set their boundaries and discuss what they expected of one another.

I proceeded back upstairs and met with the British High Commission liaison. I requested that the delegates who would be staying at the guesthouse be pointed out, allowing me to introduce myself and to invite them to see the suites in which they would be staying. I took each delegate to his or her suite, using much the same routine that I had used with the Queen. Most of the time, while I was showing the delegates their suites, they would be more interested in President Mandela, how the different cultures were getting on, and what the mood in the country was.

They were speaking to a man who had lived with the president, seen how the government machine had been put together and worked with the who's who in the government. I did not have to speculate. A better ambassador for South Africa you would not find as I told them the truth of what I'd seen with all the excitement and passion in my heart. By the time I left the suites, I could feel the delegates' desire to see and experience everything I had told them about – the Madiba magic.

The first day of a state visit normally allowed all the dignitaries to settle into the guesthouse. All the other delegates who were not staying at the guesthouse were usually hosted at a hotel close to us. They, too, would have the day to rest and start prepping for the next few days, which would entail back-to-back meetings, functions and the state banquet.

Once all my guests had settled into their rooms, I would post a chambermaid outside each one in the event that a guest required anything. The lounge would be set with a full bar, exquisite snacks and fountains of fresh fruit. We would allow the delegates to enjoy the gardens, golf course, tennis courts and the superb views of Pretoria.

Police were placed every hundred metres around the perimeter, and bodyguards followed the delegates at a distance like chameleons stalking insects in the Amazon – the insects know something is there, but do not quite know where. There was also security on the roof. No one was getting in. The guesthouse's position on the crest of the hill also made it secure.

Once I was happy that everyone felt at home, I went to the kitchen and started prepping for dinner. I had already asked the Queen where

Queen Elizabeth II gave me this signed photo when she and Prince Philip left the guesthouse.

they would be dining, so I was prepping for thirty-two delegates in the main dining room and the Queen and the Prince in their suite. The first day was always the calm before the storm.

Later that evening, when the delegates arrived from the hotel and the High Commission to join their colleagues for dinner, I welcomed them at the front door and escorted them to the lounge for pre-dinner drinks. I then went to announce to the delegates in our suites that their guests had arrived. The delegates in our suites would always be presidents, deputy presidents and ministers.

When the pre-drinks session was over, I escorted all the delegates to the dining room where they would be treated to the best of South African food and drink. We would spoil them to the hilt. At any given time, I could receive the call to say that the Queen and Prince were ready to dine. I then multitasked, and served both venues according to their timeframes.

Once dinner was over, the guests proceeded up to their suites. Then, the worker bees came out. The staff from the United Kingdom went down to their cars and transports, and started carting up files, computers and printers. They all had mobile offices. I set them up in the far offices, allowing them to start their daily duties.

Through all of this, we used a coded language of speaking to one another in extremely quiet voices that we accompanied by hand signals and gestures. If you had to turn the sound off at a beatbox show while all the beatboxers were trying to outdo each other, you'd get the picture.

Once all the office staff had settled, the dining rooms were clean and the lounge had been freshened, I sent the first shift home and the second shift arrived. I placed them outside the offices; every now and then, they would freshen the drinks station and see whether there were any requirements.

This was my gap. I went upstairs and soaked the layers of duty out of my body, and washed all the doubts and concerns I had about the following day out of my hair. Once I was squeaky clean and new, I got dressed in my suit for the following working day. The best part was going to sit with my boys as they slept on, gently brushing their hair to one side and telling them how great they would be one day –

that they were going to change the world for the better, and must never forget the love and bond that we had. I went to sit next to my wife as she slept, gently placing my hand on her soft, pure skin. She gave me half a glance and curled around me like a cat on a Persian rug in front of a fireplace in the middle of winter.

I waited for her beautiful head to slip back onto the pillow as her dreams embraced the clouds, and carefully manoeuvred off the bed. I then went downstairs and sat on one of the high-backed chairs, propped a pillow under my head and closed my eyes for a two-hour rest session.

I always pictured myself as a Formula One car stopping for a pit stop; in that short time, I could be refuelled and hydrated, good to go to win the next few laps.

'Chef, would you like a deep or soft tissue massage?' I heard as I looked over the soft bed I was lying on to see the ocean waves breaking on the white sand in a smooth rhythm. The cool breeze that whispered off the sea was as gentle on my skin as thousands of butterfly wings.

'Deep tissue please, yes, deep tissue.'

'What, Chef? You want a deep tissue? Are you mad? I asked how many sugars you want in your coffee.'

I sat up, yearning to go back to my avatar.

'Chef, you okay?'

One of my staff members stood looking at me, holding a tray with freshly brewed filter coffee on it for me.

'Thank you. What time is it?'

'Just before five. The office staff are packing up.'

'Good. I'll go see to them now.'

I savoured every sip of the coffee, trying to get my body to extract all the caffeine from each sip to charge me.

I stood up and went to the bathroom, ensured I looked just as fresh and crispy as I had after my bath, put a friendly smile on my face, drew my shoulders back, beamed my personality and – let's go!

I walked around the offices, speaking to the worker bees, checking up on them to ensure they had all they needed. I informed them that breakfast would be served in the main dining room at 6 a.m. Most importantly, I poured sympathy onto them for the long hours they worked. I told them I was certain they were appreciated, and that all the work they did was the backbone of the meetings, and that, without them, the state visit would not be a success. I was a crystal ewer, dispensing water to the dehydrated where they lay in the desert sun.

Once the mobile offices had been taken back to the transports and cars, my team reset the offices for the day's meetings. I served all the worker bees breakfast before they retired to their hives to rest. That night, they would start collecting pollen again for their queen.

I then ushered the guesthouse guests into their private dining room for breakfast. They could have silver service in their suites, if they chose. After breakfast, I informed the delegates that their staff was waiting to brief them about their night's work.

After breakfast, the events of the day started all over again.

THE DAY BEFORE THE STATE BANQUET, a whole delegation from the British High Commission came to see me. There was a full inspection of all the fresh produce, crockery and cutlery I was going to use. I had the florist make up samples of the bouquets, and we revisited the drinks list and the order of proceedings. I took the whole delegation through the motions of where the president would meet the Queen, which passages they would walk down, how they would enter the banquet hall, and the routes the waiters would walk to serve the food, and how they would clear.

Then, in a very thick British accent: 'Chef, I see two problems that we have no choice but to resolve immediately.'

'Please, sir, point them out so we can rectify them and ensure that everything runs perfectly.'

The gentleman stood with his index finger and thumb latched onto his chin, looking at the ceiling as if awaiting words from above. We all looked at him, thinking, *Come on, get on with it. We haven't got all bloody day.*

'The Queen does not use a fish knife. The place setting will have to be changed.'

I walked to the mock table in the Banquet Hall and removed the fish knife, reset the cutlery and spaced it perfectly again. I waited for a standing ovation, thinking, *Okay, problem one solved. Next? We have a full agenda. I cannot bloody stand here all day.*

It looked as if the gentleman was now adding something up on an abacus in the air. 'We cannot have the entrée carried from the kitchen to the Banquet Hall. The distance is too great. I fear that it could be contaminated.'

'Sir, if I may, I make the entrées in a room that is set at fifteen degrees Celsius. They are made fresh. I place a cloche over each plate straight away, and it is immediately taken out.'

'I don't like it. The food is carried for over seventy metres. It *must* come from a closer area.'

We then walked to adjacent rooms to see whether we could plate the entrées in them, but none of the rooms met kitchen hygiene standards. We were getting frustrated. I walked outside to the eastern quad next to the Banquet Hall.

'What if I serve from here?'

'How are you going to do that?'

'I will park an eight-ton refrigerated truck here, and serve from the back of it. The food will be only eight metres from the Banquet Hall.'

Everyone was impressed – there were smiles all around. The High Commission was finally content with the banquet arrangements.

As I waved them goodbye and their transport drove down the

driveway, my head started shouting at me: 'You asshole! You *moron*! Open your mouth so you can take your foot out of it.' Besides the fact that I had to coordinate the guesthouse all day and the meetings that were to be held there, that the president and the Queen were around, that I had to cook lunch for everyone and serve it in different venues, prep all the food for the state banquet, check all the suites to ensure they were perfect, feed all the security staff and attend meetings myself, I now had to find a truck, get it to the Banquet Hall side, set it up as a kitchen, get all the *mise en place* into the truck, then move, with my team, between the different kitchens to serve different courses.

I would rather have put my dick in a liquidiser.

During the day's duties, I was able to phone Joe Schanding, a friend who owned a catering company called VIP Caterers, and ask whether I could borrow an eight-ton truck for the next two days. Being the great man he was, he sent the truck over on banquet day. When it arrived, George, the driver, got out; I walked with him along the dirt road that was on the edge of the cliff at the back of the guesthouse.

'No, boss. The truck won't fit here.'

'Please, George. It has to. I need it that side.'

'No, boss. Really.'

'Okay, George. How does R200 sound? I will walk in front of the truck and watch the wheels the whole time.'

George walked to the edge of the road, where the rocks were precariously held together by loose gravel and a few weeds. He picked up a rock, then threw it over the edge. I was under the impression he was thinking about it. He picked up another rock, and threw that one over the edge too.

'George ... what are you doing?'

'Boss, I'm thinking how long I've got to jump out of the truck if it falls off the edge.'

'Come on, George. It won't fall. Go fetch it.'

A few minutes later, the truck came trundling down the dirt road.

I stood in front of the truck like I was guiding an Airbus to its parking bay. Slowly, the truck started the hair-raising stretch of road. Its right side was brushing the back wall of the Banquet Hall. As I crouched down, I could see that the inner tyre was on the road – but the outer one was in the air. I stood up. George, sweating and jittery like a raccoon cornered in a house, was looking in all directions at the same time. He pointed at me shakily, then gave me a thumbs-up to ask if everything was okay. I smiled and threw him two thumbs. 'All perfect! We are halfway,' I said, my throat trying to keep my heart from jumping out of it.

Between my micro-second heartbeats, the back of the truck slipped towards the cliff edge. George jumped out the passenger window and almost landed in my arms. The truck stalled, lurching closer to the rocks that George had thrown off the edge.

'Fuck!' I shouted.

George was trying to speak while gesturing with his whole body that he was not going near that truck. I walked to the front to see how I was going to do this. As I tried to climb onto it, the truck moved – not much, but enough to tell me what was going to happen next.

I walked briskly to the side door, wanting to shoot through the passage to the back door and call security to see whether they had any advice. As I stepped into the passage, a bodyguard rushed up to me.

'Are you okay, Chef?'

'Yes – why?'

'It looks like you've had a heart attack! You are soaking wet and in a mess. Look at your shoes!'

I told him the story and asked if he had any advice, begging him to keep it discreet. He thought for a while. 'Don't worry, Chef. I've got your back.' He grabbed his radio *'Boet*, Chef is in *kak*. He needs us at the back of the Banquet Hall.'

'I asked you to keep it discreet!'

'I thought you wanted help!'

Like a herd of buffalo, the bodyguards came storming down the passage towards us. If they had thundered any louder, the delegates would think the guesthouse was under attack. I shook my head and walked towards the truck, the herd in tow.

As they walked around the corner, a few of them said in unison, '*Jy is in groot kak*. (You are in deep shit.)'

I turned to them and said, coolly, 'Thank you for your great observation.'

The guys walked around the truck and looked underneath, and from all sides. One bodyguard had gone up onto the guesthouse roof. '*Boet*, it looks even *kakker* from up here.'

Eventually, one of them turned to me: 'My wife's brother is a tow-truck driver. I'll call him.'

I don't kiss men, but almost kissed him. He called, and informed me that his brother-in-law would be there in an hour.

I went upstairs and tried to freshen up, then went into the chiller, at minus twenty-five degrees, to freeze all the worry out of me as I tried to bring my body temperature down. Over the radio, I heard that the Queen was looking for me. Just what I needed: I'm sweaty and stressed, and one of the most important people in the world wants to speak to me. I walked through the kitchen and sprayed on a bit more cologne to try mask the smell of stress.

I went down to the front door, which was where I was being called from. The door was ajar. As I peeked through it, I could see the Queen speaking to the press. Our in-house security was reassuring me that everything would be fine and that, when the tow truck came, they would deal with it. The door swung open and the Queen stepped back inside.

'Afternoon, young man. Thank you so much for all you are doing for our delegation. Your food really is wonderful. May I ask for a light lunch, and to show me where I will be meeting President Mandela this evening prior to the banquet?'

The Queen removed her large hat and started to go upstairs. I heard her mumbling about the press. Not sure what she was saying, I just replied, 'I can believe you, Your Majesty.'

I explained that I would fetch President Mandela at the front door and escort him to the foot of the stairs, where we were standing now. I would run upstairs beforehand and notify the royal couple about how many minutes away the president was, so that we could all meet at this spot.

I then asked her whether she would like me to escort her upstairs, but she declined; one of her aides popped out of the lounge and asked her for some time on a certain matter.

As the Queen walked over to the lounge with her beautiful, wide-brimmed hat, I realised I'd just been speaking to the Queen of England. She was sweet and caring, with a warm family feel about her – obviously very well spoken, yet I'd felt like I was speaking to my gran. How does all that power and influence fit into one lovely, caring lady? I wondered. I'd been so busy doing my duties that it had taken a day or two for me to stop and smell the roses. At that moment, I saw myself from the outside and recognised how honoured and privileged I was to be able to have the aura of people like the Queen rub off on me. It was as if I took on a bit of power from each of the famous dignitaries with whom I dealt.

As the Queen disappeared into the lounge, I heard a soft whistle. Down the passage, one of the bodyguards was waving to me as if I were about to be attacked by a shark in the ocean. 'Come quickly! Run, man!'

He turned and ran through the pool room. I followed.

There stood a toothless wonder with a smile on his face. 'This is where the Queen is staying! I saw it on TV!'

'Hi! Great to meet you. Thank you for helping me out. If you get this right, I will invite you and your family for a tour when there are no guests staying here.'

A bit of motivation couldn't be a bad thing.

We walked to the back of the truck. The tow-truck driver bent over the back of his rig, showing us his ass-smile in all its glory. Nothing like the crack of dawn; all the bodyguards looked away.

He placed a large bag under the refrigerated truck and started to inflate it. When the truck had been brought level, he hitched it to his rig and started pulling.

'Wait wait wait! What are you doing?'

'Saving your truck!'

'But I need it on the other side – don't take it away!'

He climbed out of his rig with a squint look on his face, the creases on his forehead making a maze for the beads of his sweat to try to escape. He slammed the door and walked around the Banquet Hall; from the back of the truck, I could see his long socks, pulled aggressively over his calves, and dirty brown leather shoes pace up and down at the front of the truck. He bent down in different places and looked under the truck. They may say 'God Save the Queen', but I'd rather He saved the poor people who were standing on that side from witnessing his hairy butt peering out from the top of his denim shorts.

He walked back to me, then looked at me with a face as serious as it could get.

'Listen to me. This truck is *only* going backwards. Forwards: no bloody way.'

I was getting desperate. 'Please, I beg you. You name it, I will give it to you. But please, please help.'

'Sorry, but no. And you still owe me a tour.'

He went to the back of the truck, deflated his bag, threw it on the back of his rig, got in, and sped off like the cartoon roadrunner.

So, there I was – still stuck. I *had* to get the truck to the other side. One of the guesthouse security guards cruised up to us. He was such a smoothie, without a doubt the coolest security guard I had ever seen.

'Let's phone the captain and ask for a helicopter. I saw a few land when I was on my way in this morning.'

'Please, if you can arrange this I will buy you guys and the captain a case of whisky.'

The next thing he was on the phone, arranging everything. When I heard him offer the captain three bottles of whisky, I got in his face, gesturing for him to offer more. I would do anything to make this happen.

He ended the call. 'Chef, you said two cases of whisky. I'll take both and make it happen. How I do it is up to me.'

I agreed, and stepped back.

The bodyguards formed a huddle, looking like they were about to make the final play for a try. I inched closer. I could hear them radioing different police divisions, reporting that there was going to be a training exercise at the Presidential Guesthouse for the state banquet and that air support should be ignored during the test.

I went back to the kitchen to prep for the light lunch the Queen had requested – she did not want a big meal before the state banquet. I had sent the food to her suite and got back to prepping for the banquet when I heard a helicopter. I ran outside: the wind was gusting and the sand was stinging my hands and face and I felt it caking on my face. It was music to my ears, peace to my soul. I could not quite see what they were doing – it was all happening behind the Banquet Hall and I could not get any closer. I went inside to ensure that all the windows were closed, and that the helicopter was not making any of our guests uneasy. By the time I reached the end of the passage near the offices, I heard the helicopter flying away. I took a very brisk walk to the east side of the Banquet Hall.

There stood the truck, in all its glory. I wanted to hug it.

I ran around high-fiving all the bodyguards, as if I had scored the try after their huddle. Needless to say, they all ate like kings that day. I treated *them* like royalty.

(Years later, I spoke to a chef who had worked in Cape Town for the second president of democratic South Africa. He did not like me much, despite my liking him – he is a great guy. He threw what happened that day in my face, to try to embarrass me. It made me realise that the things that happen behind the scenes are the best things to remember. Yes, it was embarrassing – but, hell, I would do it all over again.)

I got the truck washed. The cleaning crew cleaned up around the Banquet Hall, and the gardeners pruned the shrubs and wiped the dust off the flowers. We drew near to completing the hall for the state banquet: the red carpets came out and were brushed, the windows were cleaned, the walls were wiped over and over again. The kitchen was buzzing, security continuously checking everything, the British delegation asking incessant questions and checking everything according to their notes, then asking and checking again.

Time was marching by like the Queen's Guard changing shifts back at her palace. I looked up at the clock. The hands told me it was time to go and get ready myself. I sent my whole team to freshen up and change into their formal uniforms. While I was upstairs changing, all the things that still had to happen sped through my head like comets.

Back downstairs, all the metal detectors were in place and the security forces were busy with their final sweeps before handing the Banquet Hall over to me. It was eerie – when security withdrew, there was no one left. Just me, doing my final checks and walking around the empty tables. When I stood in each corner of the Banquet Hall, all the tables, with their cutlery and glasses, formed a pattern of perfection. As I walked from corner to corner, the patterns would seem to dance on the tables, with each item positioned in the same place on each table.

The carpets told a story of who had been there and in which direction they had gone, so they were brushed again. It was all perfect, ready to host two of the most famous and highly ranked people in the world. We had done all we could to show the world how great South Africa was and to show the Queen how much love and respect each one of us had for our president.

Protocol arrived, and I handed the hall over to John Reinders. His team's job would now begin, by welcoming all the guests and seating them. They ran the logistics of the state banquet.

The radio crackled, telling me that the president was fifteen minutes out, and I went upstairs to inform first the Queen and then all her staff who were staying at the guesthouse. The staff would leave first, and head towards the Banquet Hall. Soon, President Mandela was five minutes away. I went upstairs to give the Queen an update. Then the radios started to chatter like birds being stalked by a snake.

'President's convoy has entered the gate.'

I ran upstairs and informed the Queen, then bolted down to the front door to meet him.

'Evening, young man,' the president greeted me as he climbed out of the car.

'Evening, my president. Welcome back to the guesthouse.'

'Yes, my home away from home. Is the Queen ready?'

'Yes, my president.'

I escorted the president in and assisted him up the stairs. Mary then took his side as I ran up the stairs to escort the Queen.

I met them just before they reached the stairs: 'Your Majesty, you look exquisite. Prince Philip, you look amazing.'

I got two warm smiles, which I looked past at the sparkling crown that haloed over the Queen's head and all the medals standing at attention on the Prince's chest.

'President Mandela has arrived and is waiting downstairs.'

As we reached at the bottom of the stairs, the President greeted the royal couple and off they went towards the Banquet Hall. I remember standing and watching them as they slowly glided down the passage, knowing I was watching history in the making.

My front-of-house duties were done.

When the banquet was over, and all its honoured invitees had left, everyone at the guesthouse was pleased with how the day had gone. The hall was being cleaned, and the red carpets were rolled up, ready to welcome guests another day. All the crockery, cutlery and glasses were being packed back into the safe, ready to rest after their shining display, knowing that they were safe on their sturdy shelves. I went to chat to the British staff who were packing up and prepping for the Queen's departure the next day. Their weary movements and red eyes served as a map of their efforts over the past few days. As they moved slowly up and down the stairs to the transports, I assisted where I could, as my team were all busy with their duties.

With the African sun starting to come out, I went upstairs to freshen up and change my suit. I served the last breakfast to the visiting staff. As they finished and departed, hugs and kisses were shared, with promises of seeing one another again if there was another such visit. I sent the Queen and Prince their breakfast and fed all the in-house dignitaries. My team was pushing to finish; they, too, had been working hard for the past few days while their families had yearned for togetherness.

When the time came for the grand departure, certain people were asked to go and see the royal couple. I was one of them. We were called in and thanked in person for our service. The Queen and the Prince handed me two envelopes, one for me and one for the staff, with a gratuity to thank us. The Queen handed me a photo that she had personally autographed.

I then went to say goodbye to each person who had stayed at the guesthouse, and made my way downstairs to await the royal couple. We had some fun with the media, opening the front door to get the cameras flashing and closing it again to hear sighs of disappointment.

As the guests started moving down the stairs, I knew the time had come. They took their places in the convoy, then the Queen's bodyguards led the royal couple down. I received my final thank you and handshake. The Queen straightened herself up a little more as the Prince braced; the doors opened and the media went into action.

Just like that, several days had passed, and the royal convoy's V8s roared away to the main gate, the media disappearing with the sound.

I shook in-house security's hands and gave them one of the cases of whisky for assisting with the truck. They'd get the other case when the truck was back on the west side of the Banquet Hall. I locked the front door, then went through the whole guesthouse and double-checked that my team had locked everything up. I gave the staff their gratuity and asked them to split it equally.

Not long afterwards, I heard a loud disagreement in the staff room. When I stuck my head around the corner, I could see the team shouting at David, one of the cleaners.

'What's going on here? We are all tired. Let's just finish up, please.'

'Chef, David has been drunk for two days. He does not deserve any of the tip.'

When I walked in, I saw how intoxicated he was. He could hardly sit on the chair. I asked why this had not been brought to my attention; as I looked around, the whole team seemed sheepish. I phoned the Department of Foreign Affairs' HR and told them the story. They advised me to have him escorted off the estate – they would deal with the matter the next working day. I informed the staff what was the procedure and got a police officer to escort him outside the gates.

Finally, I was alone. The only thing between me and my bed was a huge hug from my boys and a sweet kiss from my wife.

Then: 'Chef! Chef, howzit? How are you?'

Why did I not lock the door? I shouted at myself in my head. I faked a smile and turned around. Some of the bodyguards had gathered, with a few beautiful girls.

'You see! I *told* you I knew the Executive Chef of South Africa! Chef, tell them who just left! Tell them!'

I told them a few stories, then whispered to one of the bodyguards that I was dead tired and just wanted to get some sleep. I'd had nine hours' sleep in the past five days. He begged me to have just one drink with them, then they would leave. I went upstairs to fetch the drinks. To my wife's disgust that they expected this from me, and that I allowed it, I went back downstairs.

I sat there listening to the war stories the guys were telling the girls, trying to impress them. They had one idea in mind, and enjoying the whisky was not it. I quickly finished my drink. As I looked at these girls – who had spent many an hour getting ready to come to the guesthouse and were dying for me to say a few things – with no notice, no warning, no letter or call, I farted loudly. I was so tired – half in a coma – that I had not even known that it was coming.

Let me tell you, that screwed up *that* moment. The guys laughed nervously, and the girls did not know where to look.

I stood up, greeted everyone, told them to leave their glasses on the stairs, and announced that I was going to bed. I locked the door and went upstairs. Nine hours' sleep in five days. I was going to *punish* my bed: I took off my shoes and fell onto it. I vaguely remember my wife undressing me and putting my PJs on, then I slept for over twenty hours.

I spent the next few days with my family.

Back at work, we started the whole process again: airing, cleaning, polishing and prepping the guesthouse for the next state visit.

Just before lunch, I walked past the dining room to find David sitting and speaking to a gentleman from the Department of Foreign Affairs' legal team.

'Sorry, why are you here without my permission?' I asked.

'I am here to charge you with racism. So no, I don't need to notify you.'

WTF? I was racking my brain for evidence of my ever having been racist.

'Excuse me? On what grounds?'

I was asked to sit down, which I did. With panic in my voice, as I knew I was being charged without evidence, I said, 'Can I see the charges, please? Surely I have the right?'

Jean Lombard, the guesthouse office secretary, stepped into the room: 'Sorry, Chef. I need to speak to you. It's extremely urgent.'

I stood up and wanted to tell her what was going on – right at that moment, *this* was urgent.

Then Mary stepped into the room, eating an apple. Her voice was stern: 'Chef, I have been phoning you. Why have you not been answering?'

Now, more than ever, I felt like I had been set up. I just wanted to run. Being accused of racism is very serious – I'd rather kill someone than be a racist. If Mary was involved, this had to be serious shit. All the moisture in my mouth seemed to drain down to my sweaty hands.

'The president has just arrived. He was at the Union Buildings for a meeting and wanted to stop here for lunch before his next meeting. Is there food ready?'

Standing between Mary and a firing squad, I realised that Mary was not aware of what was happening. Before I could answer her, she looked at the lawyer: 'What are you doing here?'

'Brett Ladds is under investigation for being a racist.'

'Who charged him?'

'David [name withheld].'

Mary stepped out of the room and came back a few minutes later. I could hear the pressure in the room forcing the clock's second hand back, making the whole process feel like it was going on forever. The president was on her heels. Now, not only did I have a member of Foreign Affairs' legal team in the dining room, I also had

Mary and the president. My zip could have been down and I would not have cared.

'This man is no racist. I am sure the charges have no substance. If there are any other issues, they will go through Mary. This meeting is over.' Then, looking at me, the president said, 'Chef, could you please make me something light to eat? And a fresh fruit salad for afterwards, please?' He sat down, and I turned to the kitchen.

Mary shouted down the passage, 'Don't forget lunch for me, Chef!'

Again – WTF? I saw the lawyer walk out while I was busy with lunch, so I ran up behind him to speak to him. 'Sorry, sir, but I feel the way you handled this was wrong. You could at least have given me a chance and spoken to me in private. Instead, you charged me immediately. I could lose my job over something like this. Just know one thing: of all the cases you have taken, I'm sure you will *never* forget this one. Just remember who my witness was.'

I went back to the kitchen and served the president and Mary separately. The president left to go back to the Union Buildings; after a while, Mary came to sit in the kitchen and speak to me. She told me that she'd spoken to David and the lawyer about the charges. David had laid a charge of racism against me to derail my charging him for drinking on duty. He planned to use the charge as a bargaining chip against me to drop my case.

I thanked Mary for her help. And charged David, nonetheless; he was given a final warning.

TWO YEARS LATER, in November 1997, I had the honour of having another royal, Prince Charles, stay with us at the Presidential Guesthouse for a state visit.

Prince Charles was given a running start when he visited South Africa. On his arrival, he had no time to freshen up, relax and take a breather – the British High Commission had informed us that it would be hosting a high tea for the prince, with selected guests, in the guesthouse gardens.

We set up for the tea. The tables and flowers were fitting for the occasion, with silver five-tier stands full of the most exquisite finger foods, pastries and cakes.

Me, personally? I suggested: when in Africa, do as we do. I wanted to host an upmarket sunset braai, but I lost that vote. High tea it was.

All the ladies were dressed in hats and high heels and stockings; the gentlemen wore waistcoats and blazers. One problem, though: they were dressed for high tea in the United Kingdom, not for the African summer sun. By the time the Prince arrived, our guests had turned from a lighter shade of pale to a redder shade of pink.

The Prince was a gentleman, spending time at each table and greeting all his guests. After a while, he came to me and asked me whether I would take him to his suite. I started escorting him to the guesthouse, not knowing what to say – so I walked in front like a guide.

'Sorry, Chef,' he said, as that is how I had introduced myself, 'is there any way you could take me to the guesthouse that's not through the front door?'

'Yes, sir. Let's go around the back – the doors are open on the veranda.'

The prince started speaking to me as we walked. He was so easy to speak to, and had a great sense of humour.

When we walked onto the veranda, we saw a cleaner who was in the process of sweeping up the light bit of dust that had settled from the breeze that was blowing up the hill. The Prince stopped and looked at the cleaner: 'I can see there has been a major change in your country. The last time I was here, you had small mops. Look at those long-haired mops now!'

I laughed nervously, not sure whether I was being tested.

Upstairs in his suite, I gave him the tour, as I had done for his mom and would do for all the other royals and presidents who would stay there. When I heard how he spoke to his staff, and how they respected him in return, I realised that he must be a great man. Prince Charles taught me great lessons just by being himself.

Seeing Prince Charles off on his way to one of his excursions.

The media is exceedingly harsh on public figures. From what I had read and researched, I expected to find myself dealing with a very prim and proper man. He was completely the opposite: despite his exalted title, here was a man who was loved by all who dealt with him. His sense of humour was remarkable and his knowledge could teach Wikipedia a few things. When I think back to that state visit, I recall there never being a dull moment. Every time he opened his mouth, everyone would lean in to hear what he had to say and the authority with which he would say it.

The Prince ate every meal in the dining room. I would stay in the room just to listen to the conversations he'd have with his power team, who really knew their jobs. I never heard him criticise or talk down to anyone – he would guide and advise everyone he spoke to in a way that made that you feel that you were somebody. His was one of my most memorable visits.

His gift to me when he left was a beautiful collector's bottle of whisky – white porcelain, with his family emblem on it. When I received it, I hugged it all the way to my wing of the house, where I put it in the display case in my bar. Just think of the stories I would tell people while we admired that bottle, and drank from it at my sons' twenty-first birthday parties …

Except that, immediately after the state visit, Drugs and Animal – friends from Witbank – and my brother arrived for a visit of their own. I asked them to excuse me for a few hours so I could have a nap before we braaied – I was always dead tired after a state visit. Off I went to the bedroom; I closed the door and went to sleep.

Much later that night, laughter and the sound of running up and down the passage woke me up. I went to the lounge to find my friends and brother tag-wrestling on the couch. My wife apologised to me profusely. She'd been trying to keep them quiet, as she knew I needed the rest. I gave her a kiss and thanked her for loving me so much. I could see that the guys were in no state to be reasoned with. When they saw me, they got so excited that they did a monkey dance. I smiled and tried to chase the sleepy feeling away.

They gave me a Coke and said they'd kept it for me. I downed it, then another, and another – and started getting into the groove. We ended up on the roof with a bonfire, drinking and laughing the night away.

The next morning, once Tracey had spoilt us with coffee, we ate toast until the bread was finished. We got dressed and went shopping for that night, so we could have a rerun.

When we got home and everything was ready for the braai, I invited my friends and my brother to the bar and stood behind it like a boss. I started telling them how well I had got on with Prince Charles and what an admirable man he was. Then, I told them that he had given me a gift – a collector's bottle of whisky – in person, and that I would celebrate my sons' twenty-first birthdays with it. I'd rehearsed this story.

But I started getting annoyed: I expected them to share in my excitement and be happy for me. Hell, how many people could say that the Prince of Wales had given them a bottle of whisky? Why had they gone so quiet?

'Am I boring you? Really, if you don't feel happy for me you could at least act it. I can live with that.'

Drugs looked straight at me. 'Please don't tell me it's the white bell-shaped bottle.'

'Yes – why?'

'Uh … that's what we were all drinking in the Coke last night.'

All I could do was walk out of the bar to the bedroom and slam the door.

A bit later they asked if they could come in and speak to me. I advised them it was not a good idea – after all, I'd gone to the bedroom to stop myself from hitting them. To make matters worse, they said that they'd been drunk so I couldn't blame them that the bottle had looked nice. The collector's bottle. Given to me by a member of the royal family.

That blew my lid. I tore open the door and chased them out of the guesthouse like the dogs I thought they were. They jumped into a car and left. Close to tears, I went upstairs and took the bottle down. My wife walked in and said that had she known she would have stopped them.

I lay on the carpet, removed the cork and tried to get the last few drops to drip onto my tongue. I got a few, and made like I was savouring all the unique flavours Prince Charles had told me about. I knew I was bullshitting myself.

Several hours later, they came back. I heard them whistling for my wife.

'Is it safe?'

'Yes, come up – looks like he's over it.'

They came up with a few bottles of whisky that looked similar, and said they'd been to every bottle store in town to try to replace it. I told them I was over it – that all I had wanted was to taste it, and that, of course, they could shove all the whisky they'd bought up their asses.

After a few drinks, we were all brothers again and had a great time, which didn't stop me reminding them about what they'd done at every get-together we've had since … without Drugs, that is.

Greg Rogers – the name his parents gave him, and whom I'd known since hostel in Standard Six – died in a collision with a truck that left a wife, a son and an unborn baby.

Miss you, my friend. Until we drink Prince Charles' whisky together in heaven …

9
From Russia to the Vatican – with love

On the day the Russian delegates arrived at the guesthouse, we were not disappointed. They fitted the stereotype to a T – they were large, well-built, blond, and all had the same look on their faces: mess with me and I will kill you. When our South African bodyguards got out of their cars as the convoy stopped at the guesthouse, it was always impressive to see their bulky frames. But when the Russian delegation got out after them, it looked as if the Russians were there to protect the South Africans!

I escorted the main delegates upstairs. Once I'd given each delegate a tour of his suite, I went down to the front door, where I found a short, chubby Russian with stubble and glasses. He was trying to communicate something to a member of guesthouse security. I stood behind him to see whether I could help.

'Sorry, sir, what are you looking for?' asked the policeman.

'Looking for shshshshsh,' the Russian said, spittle flying as he used his hands to show what looked like water coming out of a shower head.

'Sir, there are showers upstairs. The Chef can show you, in your suite.'

'No, no, no! Not shower – I want shshshshsh,' he said persistently. The policeman was getting irritated, so I jumped in. 'Can I help you, sir?'

'Yes, yes, yes, want shshshshsh,' he repeated.

At this point, I heard a voice coming out of the room where security rested.

'*Gaan bad in die rivier!* (Go bath in the river!)'

Now, I was trying to help the gentleman *and* keep a straight face.

'*Gaan was jou vuil tone in die rivier, jou vuilgat* (Go wash your dirty toes in the river, you dirty-ass),' the voice continued.

I popped my head into the room. '*Manne, asseblief. Ek sukkel hier en julle help nie.* (Guys, please. I am struggling here and you are not helping.)'

Keeping a straight face was getting more difficult by the minute. I decided to go find someone from the Russian embassy to assist me with the gentleman's request. I used hand signals to show him to follow me, but by the time I walked into the lounge he was gone.

While I'd been speaking to the chubby Russian, I noticed their security team carrying boxes and boxes up the stairs to the suites. After a while, this started to look suspicious. I pointed it out to our security, and asked whether there was any way we could check what was in the boxes. I was informed that the area upstairs was seen as part of the visiting delegation's embassy. They had diplomatic status and I was the only person who was allowed to go there, so there was nothing the team could do.

After seeing the size of the Russian delegation, I went to the kitchen and doubled the portions of meat and starch I was going to serve them. When I'd pass one of them walking around in the guesthouse, I almost felt I had to apologise for being in their space, then fall on the floor and beg them not to eat me.

Later that day, the Russian aide from the embassy came to ask whether we had swimming towels and tennis racquets and balls, as some members of their delegation wanted to enjoy the outdoors. I obliged, fetched everything they needed, and sent my team to go put it out in the required places.

True as nuts, the next moment they walked out of the front door carrying those same brown boxes. Off they went to play tennis; some of them went to lounge around the pool. After a while, you could hear laughter. It sounded like they were all having a great time. It was really amazing to hear people enjoying themselves around the guesthouse – in fact, it was the first time I'd ever heard this.

I continued cooking and prepping for dinner, then went to the suites to double-check the turndowns and confirm dinner times. The delegates who had remained inside were relaxed and had no schedule to keep to. On the way down the stairs, I caught a glimpse of the tennis court. A group of guys were lying on the court and not moving.

I walked past the security office and asked two of the guys to follow me to the pool and tennis court. One of them was the same guy who had chirped the chubby Russian earlier that morning. When we reached the tennis court, there was so much debris lying around – several large tins and glass bottles – that it looked as if a chemical bomb had been dropped. One smell of a bottle and I understood what had happened; it smelt like pure spirits. In the oversized tins (take a sardine tin and put it on steroids), I saw leftovers of fish in oil.

I asked the guy who had chirped the Russian to help me. We collected all the empty bottles and tins that were on the court and around the pool, and threw them away.

I now knew exactly what had been in those boxes.

When we got to the front door, Mr Shshshshsh was waiting for us. He started the same line of questioning again, this time with a teapot in his one hand. As we got closer, he smiled – he clearly thought he had found a way to get through to us.

'Look, look!' he said, pointing to the steam coming out of the spout. 'Want shshshshsh …'

I stepped forward. 'Sir, would you like me to make your shower warmer?'

Maybe he wanted more pressure and heat in his shower.

Then, '*Ek het klaar vir jou gesê, vat jou vuil gat en gaan bad in die rivier. Jou vuil gat sal die bokke stroomaf doodmaak* (I told you already to take your dirty ass and bath in the river. Your ass is so dirty it will kill all the buck downstream).'

'*Asseblief, manne. Ek wil hom help* (Please, guys. I want to help him),' I said.

'*Fokkof en gaan eet vis* (Fuck off and go eat fish).'

Security was not helping at all. I felt so bad at this stage that I escorted the gentleman to the aide, making sure he did not disappear this time. After a brief chat, the aide explained that he was looking for … a sauna. Finally, we knew what he was after! I told him we didn't have a sauna at the guesthouse, but that I could arrange for him to use the one at the gym I went to. I promptly got security to take him there.

I was back in the kitchen when my wife called me to the window that overlooked the front entrance. As true as a morning glory on a honeymoon, the guys had started waking up and moving from the pool and tennis courts back to the guesthouse. Some of our security came to the window and we started taking bets on how hungover they were going to be.

I went to the suites to ask whether dinner could be served at 7:30 p.m. I went back down to ensure that the table was laid correctly, and that everything was ready. Just after 7:30, the delegates started arriving in the dining room.

Soon, before us were most of the guys who passed out on the tennis court and around the pool – fresh as daisies, and not the kind you find in cemeteries, smelling and looking like the brothers of Thor.

We walked around with wine and started offering everyone a nice glass of Hartenberg Chardonnay to go with the seared basa fish.

'No, not wine. Vodka.'

As I heard that, I ran down to the cellar to fetch our premier vodkas and placed them on a tray.

'Sirs, please see our range of vodkas. What can we pour you?'

'No, we fetch vodka.'

Off one of them went; sure enough, he brought a case of vodka back down with him. And that's what we started serving.

I got a call to say that a car was on its way up. I ran to the front door to see Mr Shshshshsh get out. I asked him in slow, broken English: 'Are you happy that you went for a sauna?'

He gave me a thumbs-up, said 'Yes sauna, nice!', and added another thumbs-up.

Again, from the peanut gallery: '*Fok, daai water moet vuil wees* (Fuck, that water must be dirty).'

I escorted the gentleman to his colleagues, and they all had a superb dinner – only leaving the dining room when the vodka was finished, obviously.

Later that night, when everything had calmed down, I decided to take my last tour and check up on all the guests before going to bed. The next day was a meeting day at the guesthouse, and there was to be a banquet, so it was going to be a long one; if I could get three to four hours' sleep, I would wake as strong as a bear.

Walking past the bodyguards' rooms, I heard laughing and female voices – not a sound I should have heard. I knocked on one of the doors. As I opened it, I saw some of my chambermaids sitting chatting to the Russians. Needless to say, they turned every colour possible and dashed out of the rooms. I was asked to come in.

When I asked how they managed to drink so much and remain standing, one of the Thors got up and told me to have a sip. I was not keen, but would have eaten dead puppies if he'd told me to, rather than getting the hammer. I took a sip. I gasped; breathing was impossible. They all started laughing and I tried to join in. A whisper of air slipped into my lungs, and I started breathing again.

'Now eat fish then take a sip.'

Yes! Please, please can I stick a hot poker up my ass, twice? I thought.

'Listen, eat fish then drink,' he insisted.

I took his knife and cut a piece of the oily fish, then took a sip of the vodka. I waited. I could breathe – it was not half bad.

'Eat fish and drink vodka is good, drink vodka like you, like a baby, you die.'

We had a good laugh and I went back to my wing in the house. When I got into bed, my wife asked, 'What the hell did you eat? You smell like death!' I told her the story and was sent to brush my teeth a few times. As I lay down, I could feel the heartburn coming, but wasn't sure if it was heartburn or the vodka eating me from the inside.

THE NEXT MORNING, the sun and I had a race to see who could get up first. As usual, I whipped it. I started my day by making a meal for the staff, then the dignitaries. I was called to the security room. There stood Mr Shshshshsh.

'*Sjef, die stinkgat wil weer gaan sauna. Sê vir hom as hy sy toonnaels sny en sy balhare terug in sy broek sit, kan hy gaan* (Chef, this stinky-ass wants to go sauna again. Tell him that if he cuts his toenails and puts his ball hairs back into his pants, he can go).'

Keeping a straight face, I showed him to the door and asked the biggest instigator to take him to the gym. Not that he could say no.

The day started as all conference days did, except that President Mandela was not there; I assumed all his meetings took place at the Union Buildings that day. We ran through the same state banquet protocol and procedures; I fetched President Mandela at the door, he met his counterpart, and off to the Banquet Hall they went. No truck this time, thank goodness.

Security was more relaxed this time, so I decided to feed them all in the breakfast room together. We set up the room and called both teams to come eat at once. The smell of testosterone outdid the fragrant bouquet coming from my food, though. All the men were acting like kids – who could eat the most, who could eat the fastest, etc.

After the meal, you could hear each side passing snotty

comments about the other. One of the South African bodyguards decided to man up: 'Vodka is weak. We drink *mampoer* in our country. Vodka we drink with Coke.'

'Okay, give me this *mampoer*,' one of the Russians countered.

'Chef, go fetch that *doringdraad* (barbed wire) *mampoer* from your cellar.'

I went down to fetch it. I would buy this spirit at a farm outside Pretoria, the Willem Prinsloo farm. It was 80 per cent proof, had no taste, and was drunk by heroes who wanted to die impressing their friends.

I took it into the breakfast room and placed it on the table. The bodyguard asked for a double shot glass. I fetched everything myself as I wanted to see how this was going to play out. The South African filled the shot glass; the Russian downed his vodka out of a mug, then slammed the mug onto the table.

'What is small glass? We drink with mug,' the Russian said, taking the *mampoer* bottle and filling the mug to the brim.

'*Dié dom fok gaan hard val* (This dumb fuck is going to fall hard).'

The Russian stood up. '*Ypa*,' he said, and downed the mug of *mampoer*. 'This is piss. Another,' he continued, filling his mug to the brim again. '*Ypa*,' he said and downed that mug too. 'You drink your piss, I drink Russian vodka.'

As all the South African bodyguards' eyes were larger than the saucers on the table, one big *boertjie* drank the double shot of *mampoer* to make sure it was the real thing. As he shot it down, his gasping and his watering eyes proved it was the original stuff.

'Now, you drink vodka,' said the Russian.

The big-mouthed South African grabbed a mug from the side table: '*Maak vol, laaitie* (Fill it up, lightweight).'

He stood loud and proud, about to take one for Team South Africa and show the Russians what we were made of. He took that mug, held it tight, lifted it to his mouth and huck, huck, huck, he did the chuck. He put the mug down, then leant against a chair like a cowboy who had just won a standoff and taken his opposition down. We watched. In no time, the chameleon came out: he turned yellow, then green, then transparent and, before we could fathom what colour he turned next, he collapsed.

'Another vodka?' the Russian asked the South Africans – who found every excuse to leave the room. A silent pact was formed that day, that no one would speak about that night again.

After we had cleared the Banquet Hall and done all our duties, we could hear the Russians still having a great time. Their culture must be amazing: they are happy most of the time.

On the day of the delegation's departure, the staff lined up to say goodbye. As we all stood shaking hands and trying to convey messages in broken English, Mr Shshshshsh came out, carrying a wooden box. He walked straight up to me and said in fluent Afrikaans, '*Dankie dat u my gehelp het en dat jy so gaaf was* (Thank you for helping me, and for being so kind).' He then handed me the box.

Next, he walked up to the security member who had made all the rude comments about him and said, '*Baie dankie vir alles. Ek het so lekker gebly* (Thank you so much for everything. I really had a nice stay).'

The security member looked as if he had seen a ghost. '*Is jy Russies of Suid-Afrikaans?* (Are you Russian or South African?)'

'*Ek is Russies, maar ek kan elf tale praat* (I am Russian, but I speak eleven languages).'

The security member dissolved like a tablet in a glass of water.

As the Russian vice president left, he stopped and thanked me for all the effort I had gone to, and for one of his best stays abroad. He handed me two dolls, and spent some time telling me the history of the dolls and that they were handmade. The time he took to do this was an honour on its own.

As the convoy sped off like racehorses trained to know their routine, we all started to laugh and take the piss out of the police officers who had enjoyed mocking the Russian. Needless to say, they did not speak to us for the next few weeks.

PORTUGAL'S PRESIDENT JORGE SAMPAIO was, and is, an excellent representative of his most beautiful country.

When the Portuguese delegation had been dropped off at the guesthouse in June 1999, and I had showed the president his suite, done the presidential tour, and showed all the ministers their suites, the president was adamant that all his staff members should have a relaxing afternoon and enjoy their beautiful surroundings.

While I was preparing that night's dinner for the delegation, the president walked in with his hands behind his back. We all stood at attention.

'Please carry on,' he said, so I looked at and nodded to my chefs, and we all continued our preparation. I kept an eye on President Sampaio as he looked around all the corners and popped his head into the cupboards.

I have had many presidents in the kitchen. You are never sure why they are there: some come to ask for food or a drink, some come to thank us after a meal, some come to speak in confidence away from other delegates, and others come just to sit and watch, but I had never had a president who seemed to inspect the kitchen before.

'Chef, do you have things under control here, and is everything ready?'

I said what anyone else would say, obviously: 'Yes, President, I am ready.'

As he stood there, a huge smile lit up his features. I could almost see a light bulb pop up above his head.

'If everything is ready and under control, Chef, please would you show me around the guesthouse and the estate?'

'That would be an honour, President.' Once again, I found myself making promises I wasn't sure I could keep.

So, we started in the main dining room. President Sampaio asked who I had served in there. He was interested in the ANC and was really enjoying my stories, in which I praised everything that had happened since the ANC had come to power.

I was honoured when President Sampaio of Portugal asked me to have a picture taken with him.

Then he asked where I stayed. I told him, and he asked whether he could see the wing where we lived, so I took him there. Then I showed him all the suites. Even though the ministers were in their suites, he knocked on their doors and asked whether we could enter. I then showed him each suite and explained who had stayed there. Once we had been through all the suites, we went down to the main office, where President Mandela had compiled his book, with Ahmed Kathrada sitting with him day and night.

The president then slowly started reading through the books that were on the shelves. Most of them were in Afrikaans. I just stood there as he did his thing.

'Chef, tell me, there was definitely a cleaner who put all these books on the shelves.'

I looked at him, totally confused, really not knowing where he was going with this.

'President, why would you say that?'

He walked over to three different shelves, taking a book off each shelf. 'You see these books? They are all put in upside down.'

I thought up a quick answer to try to counter what the president had just pointed out and avoid embarrassment on my part: 'President, I do get the books removed on a regular basis and have the shelves wiped down. Then get the books replaced.'

The president put one hand behind his back and pointed into the air with the other. 'I do agree that the shelves are clean. As I said, it's a cleaner who put the books back. I am not blaming them. I know you said you use this desk now; I would just have expected you to notice that the books are not placed the right way up.'

I had been kicked in the nuts in such a nice way that I didn't know whether to thank the president or roll on the floor in agony.

'Let's go and walk on the estate, please.'

I could not get out of the office quickly enough. I thought everything had been perfect. Dumb books.

We walked out the front door and one of our in-house security detail followed us.

'Show me the president's house, please?'

'President, it's a bit of a walk – I would say five minutes away.'

'I love to walk. Let's see what is on the estate.'

We walked west, stopping at the stables, about a hundred metres away from the guesthouse.

'President, these are the stables. They were used for horses many years ago and have since been converted into offices for the bodyguards.'

The president looked like a tourist and really seemed interested.

A bodyguard came out of his office. 'Chef, are you okay?'

'Yes, thank you. President Sampaio of Portugal has asked me to show him around the estate.'

'Corporal,' he said to the police officer behind us, 'keep your eyes peeled and change your radio channel to ours, so I can check up on you.'

'Yes, Captain.'

The president looked at the captain and thanked him.

We continued westwards. After a few minutes, we got to the house formerly called Libertas. I explained to President Sampaio that this was the official residence of President Mandela, but that he lived in Houghton in Johannesburg and that the name of the residence had changed to Mahlamba Ndlopfu, meaning 'the new dawn'. We stood there for a while as the president looked at it. He was really enjoying himself.

We then walked eastwards down the road to the gate in Eastwood Street, towards Oliver Tambo House, the deputy president's residence. I explained who the great Oliver Tambo was and his role in the struggle. When we got to the T-junction where you could turn right to the gate or left back towards the guesthouse, I persuaded the president to turn left.

As we walked, the president was very interested in who stayed where. After walking past the cricket field and the second tee on the golf course, we reached the main gate in what was then Church Street. The captain who was in charge of in-house security was standing speaking to the officer who was in charge of the dog unit. He turned around while speaking and saw me. When he noticed the president next to me, he nearly had a seizure and practically swallowed his tongue. He marched towards us, then saw one of his men behind us. He stopped and saluted President Sampaio. I explained to the captain that this president was different from the others – he wanted to walk around and look at everything. While I was doing this, President Sampaio walked over to the dogs, started patting them, and had a conversation with the officer.

In a very diplomatic way, I urged him to make his way up to the guesthouse. As we made our way back, he was asking questions the whole time, thoroughly enjoying our conversation. When we arrived in the lounge back at the guesthouse, he thanked me and asked whether he could meet all the staff the next morning. I said this would not be a problem.

Later that night, I was woken up by the bodyguards. 'Chef. Chef, Chef!'

I woke in a daze, thinking my grandfather had come back to haunt me for stealing his car when he'd gone to bed. No, seriously – when you only have a few hours to sleep, you fall into a deep sleep. When you're woken up like that, it is horrifying.

'Yes, what is it?'

'Sorry to wake you, but the president needs to speak to you. Now.'

'Tell him I will be there soon.'

'No, not that president. Our president.'

'What? Are you sure? The last I read, President Mandela was busy mediating between two African countries.'

'Come *on*, Chef. Wake up. The president wants you to phone him *now*.'

I threw on a T-shirt on and walked out of my wing wearing that and my camo boxers. As I walk through my door, someone from Foreign Affairs' European desk was standing there with a phone in his hand.

'Hi, I am—'

'Yes, Chef, I know who you are. We have never met, though.'

'Sorry about that. How can I help?'

'There is a situation that is political. I know that you are not political at all, but please phone the president,' he said, handing me the phone

I made the call, and was instructed to go and wake up President Sampaio; his Foreign Affairs minister was already up.

Before I knew it, we were all in the guesthouse office with our PJs on and I was acting as an intercom. I would be told something, then pass the message on, then await an answer and communicate it back.

The next morning – we had not even realised the time – the office door opened slowly and my wife, already dressed and with her hair still wet, peeked into the room. The look on her face was enlightening; it was as if she had just walked onto the set of a comedy show, with all of us sitting in our PJs.

Once my wife had left, I was thanked for my role. I left to bath and change, and start my state visit routine.

After breakfast, the president asked whether 'it' had been organised. I said yes, but for the life of me couldn't remember what I was supposed to organise. Then, he asked, 'Can we take the photo at the front door?'

I remembered our conversation from the previous day. I quickly contacted a friend of mine who did photography, got the staff together, and it was photo time.

When President Sampaio left the next day, I felt sad, as he had been absolutely amazing. He'd made time for all my staff, and me. I think we bonded that night, too – not that anyone would want to remember. When he left, I stood in my usual place; when he shook my hand, he placed his left hand on my shoulder and embraced me. I read up about him today, still, and know that he sewed a patch onto the quilt of my life.

WHILE I NEVER HAD THE HONOUR of having Pope John Paul II stay at the guesthouse, he visited for a day in September 1995. Prior to the Pope's visit, we laid red carpets out everywhere. There were stanchions all over the place. Special chairs were delivered and the Pope's delegation changed everything, putting their own items in place. At the end of the preparations, the guesthouse looked like the foyer of a theatre where people would queue for the doors, queue for refreshments, and even queue to see whether there may be a spare ticket for sale.

The next day, the Pope arrived with his full entourage and security. It was hard to tell who was who, as everyone was dressed so similarly. It was one of the rare times when a delegate's whole entourage was allowed in the guesthouse. Our security felt safe with it, as every ten metres there would be a representative from the Vatican. I could not help thinking that some of the guys had to be ninjas, if you think how many people would faint at the thought of the Pope walking past them. You could see these guys were not to be messed with.

The day went as planned. We were so busy running around, replenishing all the drink stations, serving snacks, feeding the security, and me having to do the forty-metre dash to the door now and then to welcome guests and escort them to their designated meeting rooms.

Still, all the real action came at the end of the day. The Pope did as most high-profile dignitaries did, and asked whether he could thank the people who had assisted him and contributed to the day while he had been there.

A list was given to one of the Pope's delegates. You could feel the tension in the guesthouse: everyone, including me, wanted to meet the Pope officially, and not just as he had arrived in a car. I felt like we were back at school and all the kids had only twenty minutes at the tuck shop; everyone was pushing to the front and trying to make themselves seen. I did not have that privilege as I was so busy running around.

Every time I walked past the lounge, I would look in and see the

Pope sitting on the most beautiful chair speaking to someone. Just being able to see him so close by was an honour – but meeting him would be something special.

When I was returning from the far office, a line started to form down the passage of everyone who had been given the nod to meet the Pope. The delegate with the list was walking up and down, ensuring that the people were standing in the same order as the one on the list.

I walked past and smiled at everyone in the queue to say well done. Meanwhile, I was thinking, *You lucky asses. You bunch of spoilt brats!*

In animal terms, it was like the story of the fox and the crow. As the crow flew over the vineyard, he saw the fox licking his lips and staring at the grapes. So, he flew a turn or two in the air and landed right next to a bunch of grapes.

'Hello, Fox. How are you? Are you hungry?'

'No, not at all. Why would you say that, Crow?'

'I saw you licking your lips and drooling over this bunch of grapes. Why don't you just ask me to clip the stem? The grapes would fall, and you could eat them.'

'If I could jump that high I would eat you for being a liar. I am not hungry and I don't want those grapes.'

As the fox walked away, the crow could hear the fox's stomach growling.

I was that fox – too proud to ask.

I went back to the kitchen and was busy there when John Reinders ran in.

'Chef, they are waiting for you.'

'Sorry, sir? Who is waiting?'

'The Pope, my boytjie. Come.'

I took my chef's jacket off, threw down my apron and fixed myself up as I slipped through the dining room, then into the Pink Room, then through the side doors to the lounge. There, I was taken to meet the Pope. He held my hand and thanked me. He was handed a small, green box that he took and placed in my hand. He then held my hand again.

Starstruck, I was asked to stand next to the Pope with John as the people on the list came to meet him and receive a green box of their own. I stood there all pigeon-chested, the smile on my face starting to cause cramps – but there was no way that smile was going anywhere.

After a while, we started getting to John's Protocol department. One by one, the Protocol staff came in to receive their gifts. There was a red-headed woman who worked in the department. She was quite sturdy, and exceptionally feisty. I really liked her – she was excellent at her job, took no shit, and you always knew where you stood with her. She was ideal for the logistics in Protocol, yet not so good at the relations part. John called her name. She walked to the main doors that led into the lounge, then stood there like a model who was waiting for her cue to start walking the ramp. She straightened her suit jacket and braced herself. You could see that this meant a lot to her, and that she had rehearsed it in her head a hundred times.

As we all stood waiting, she took her first step. Straight away, she seemed to start walking a little faster. As if in a Tom and Jerry cartoon, the red carpet formed a bubble. Her heel hooked on it and, in slow motion, this poor, lovely lady had a speed wobble and landed on her back – legs in the air, on the Pope's side, and head on the door side. The Pope turned to his aide and I heard him say, 'I've never been greeted like this before.'

She managed to pull a Ninja Turtle breakdance move to get back onto her feet, and went to meet the pope.

Well, thank goodness Protocol was the last in the queue. I could not wait to get out of there. Once everyone had had their turn, I excused myself and ran upstairs: I was killing myself with laughter. Worst of all, it could have happened to anyone. But hell – in front of the Pope!

After washing my face, biting my tongue a few times and pinching myself, I went back downstairs to help with the breakdown after the day. I stood at the door and said goodbye to the Pope. Once the whole delegation had left, I walked down the passage to call my team for the clean-up. I passed John there; as we made eye contact, it started all over again. We rolled up and down the passage, howling with laughter.

Outside our wing at the guesthouse was a window that led onto the roof of the Banquet Hall. As all South Africans do, we love braaiing. There was no other place for this to happen, as there were police patrolling the whole time – we never had any privacy. Then, we discovered this perfect braai area. The smoke went straight upwards, so no one on the estate knew what we were doing. We were the only people there, no one could see us, and the view of the whole of Pretoria was incredible – as if the galaxy had been turned upside down and we were looking down on it from above.

That particular night, I had a friend of mine, Lucas Jordaan, over for a braai. The Pope's visit had been a lot less stressful as he hadn't stayed at the guesthouse, so I wasn't as exhausted as I normally was after a state visit. We were enjoying ice-cold Windhoeks on the roof, on this warm summer evening, while trying to solve the world's problems. The ladies were in the lounge nattering away.

My wife stuck her head through the window and handed me my phone. 'Please answer your phone, lovie. It has not stopped ringing.'

As I took the phone, it started ringing again. 'Hello, Brett Ladds here. How can I help you?'

'Hello, is that Brett Ladds?'

'Yes, it's me.'

'Brett Ladds from Mandela?'

'Tell me who is speaking or I am going to turn the phone off.'

'It's Captain [name withheld] from Mamelodi Police Station.'

That got my attention. I was praying that one of the drivers had not taken a car without my permission.

'How may I help you?'

'We have a situation here in Mamelodi that we need your help with.'

'Yes, please go on.'

'A member of your staff has been shot and killed and the community will not let us take the body till you get here and see it.'

'Why would I need to see the body? I am a chef. Are you sure it's one of my staff members? I've been with them today?'

'Yes, his name is David [name withheld]. Does he work for you?'

'Yes, he does.'

As I answered, I remembered that he'd been in the photo with President Sampaio not so long ago.

The next thing, I heard a scuffle. Another voice came on the line: 'Chef, it's me, Steven. Come here now.'

'Steven, what is going on?'

'David's neighbour shot him dead. He is a policeman. If they take the body, the policeman will not be charged. If you come here, they have to charge him. I told them you talk to Madiba.'

'Okay, Steven. I am on my way. How do I find you?'

'Don't worry – I'll find you.'

That made me think about what I was about to do: drive a Kombi into Mamelodi, being white, when it sounded like there was a huge protest going on.

I went to my wife to inform her that I was going. That was my first mistake: I was told how dangerous it was, then how stupid it was. I knew she was right, but I had no choice. I had already committed.

I apologised to our friends. But Lucas said, 'Englishman, you're not going alone. I am your friend. We will go together.'

Even Lucas, an educated engineer, could see that I had no choice.

There we went, two white peas in a green Kombi pod towards Mamelodi.

The closer we got, the more and more people we could see gathering. I opened my window and heard what sounded like thousands of men chanting. The further we drove down the main road, the more aggressive the faces of the men started to look. I started to slow down as the street started filling up as word spread of what had happened.

I looked at Lucas. 'I don't know if we are doing the right thing here.'

My words were not even cold when a man jumped into the Kombi next to me, while I was driving. I got such a fright I almost jumped onto the passenger seat and pushed Lucas out the door. The man had come out of nowhere, and was right next to me in a flash.

'Chef, drive straight. Don't worry – they will move as you drive,' Steven said.

'You scared the crap out of me, Steven.'

'I told you I would find you. I was waiting on the side of the road and this is the only way in.'

I punched him on the arm. 'You're an ass.'

'I never knew you white men could get whiter. It was funny looking at you.'

As we drove, Steven gave me directions through the streets. The way the residents moved out of our way told me that Steven had some kind of influence in the area.

We got to the eye of the storm. You could tell we were there as the residents huddled closer and closer while cursing the police.

Steven told me to stop the Kombi and get out. 'Leave the keys, no one will touch the car.'

He pushed through the crowd. Once we were at the core, I could just see a circle of police surrounding the house and the body.

As soon as the captain in charge saw us, he grabbed us and

pushed us behind a police vehicle. 'You can't just stand there. You could be a target.'

Steven walked up to the captain. 'These men are safe in Mamelodi. You police, it's you who should worry.'

'Do you want to see the body?' the captain said.

'No thank you,' I said. I had no desire to do so. My stomach can't handle that shit: I can't even watch *CSI* on TV.

'Chef, you *must* see the body. You have to see how the police shot David like a dog.'

'Please could someone tell me what happened here?'

'Chef, I told you – they shot him like a dog.'

'No, Steven. There must be a reason.'

The captain walked away, then came back. 'This is one of the witnesses. She can tell you.'

The woman told me that David had been drinking all day and that, when he had come home, he had gone to the neighbour's house and had sex with the policeman's wife. Apparently, they had been having an affair for quite a while. When the policeman got home, David had tried to hit the policeman and then run; because he was drunk, he could not run far. The policeman had shot him in anger.

I thought of the story of the scorpion and the frog. You see, the scorpion can't help what he does. It's in its nature.

'Come, Chef, let me show you,' Steven urged.

I hesitantly walked towards the gate of the house. There lay David with two bullet holes in his head, just behind his ear.

'Can I please see the policeman who shot him?'

They took me to a police car. The man inside was trembling; I believe he feared the crowd more than anything else. Next to the car was a young man, who could not have been older than twenty. He was standing guard over the car. Now I was shit scared – this poor little boy was quivering with fear. Even his jaw was chattering. I walked up to him.

'Hi. Everyone calls me Chef. I can see you are scared. So am I. We are all going to leave here without a problem, okay? I will do as I am asked so this can be over.'

'Thank you, sir. I want to die I am so scared.'

'Me too, so let's just get this out of the way.'

I knocked on the car window, and it opened. I asked the policeman if he knew what he had done. All he could say was, 'Take me to jail, take me now, get me out of here, take me to jail.'

I went back to Steven and asked whether they could take the body, take the man back to the police station. I told him I would go with them to make sure he was charged. Steven agreed, and said he would go with me. The police captain could not stop thanking me.

I went back to the young man and told him it was all over. As I walked between the crime scene and the cars, the police were practically leopard-crawling, shimmying around the walls and dashing from car to car. Either I was very naive, or my fear had turned to stupidity.

The mortuary van collected the body and drove off. I got back into the Kombi to see Lucas looking whiter than Casper the Friendly Ghost. Steven got in too. I told the captain that we would follow them to the police station.

As we drove away, the crowd started thinning. I asked Steven what was going to happen at that house. He informed me that the crowd would burn it down, and that his family would have to flee. I wanted to know if there was any way to stop it; he assured me that we should just drive.

My phone rang. It was the Minister of Safety and Security, Sydney Mufamadi, asking me if I was there; one of his security detail who lived in the area had phoned him and told him what was happening. I told the minister what I knew; he told me to phone again when I reached the police station.

Once we stopped inside the police station yard, the policeman was taken to the cells and I went to the front desk. I phoned the minister, who asked to speak to the station commander. When the conversation ended, I asked Steven if I could leave. He hugged me and thanked me. At his casual 'See you tomorrow, Chef,' I gave half a wave, jumped into the car and raced out of there back to the guesthouse. The windows of the Kombi were open. I just looked at the road and drove while Lucas looked out the window. Not a word was said.

When we got back, the ladies wanted to know what had happened. We walked straight to my bar, poured a fopolo (four-finger) shot of whisky and downed it. It evaporated before it got to our stomachs. We told the ladies. Then, I put the lid on the braai, put the meat in the fridge and, with not many a word spoken, Lucas grabbed his belongings, looked at his wife and left. I remember just lying in the bath that night. Far too much for my brain.

The scorpion's body sank as it drifted downriver.

I HAD THE HONOUR of serving Prime Minister Tony Blair for several days in January 1999. He was an utter gentleman, his state banquet and state visit ran like clockwork – everything was on time, everyone was happy and he and Cherie Blair were just such a beautiful couple.

He was attentive to his spouse, and she was very much part of the delegation. The only problem when I served and dealt with the couple in person was that *they* would make *you* feel that you were doing them the favour – that's how polite and understanding they were. More of a gentleman and lady one could not find.

Taking human nature into account, when someone is always nice to you, and kind, you can expect that they see their kindness as their way of saying thank you. Ask any waiter – or maybe you have been one yourself: the kind, sweet customers are often the ones who tip poorly. It's like, 'We were nice and did not give you shit, so take that and go pay your rent and buy groceries.' People like that are asses.

10 DOWNING STREET
LONDON SW1A 2AA

THE PRIME MINISTER   13 January 1999

Dear Mr. Ladds,

I am writing to thank you and your staff for looking after Cherie and me so well during our recent stay at the Presidential Guesthouse. We are grateful for your efforts to make us so comfortable.

Yours sincerely

Tony Blair

Mr Brett Ladds

My thank-you letter from Tony Blair.

This was in no way the prime minister and his wife: he was insistent on seeing me in person prior to his departure. I received the most beautiful leather folder with '10 Downing Street' and its emblem embossed on it. I was so grateful and kept on thanking them. Cherie asked me to open the folder. Inside it was a tip (a very nice one, I might add), a letter thanking me, and some stunning smalls from the United Kingdom.

Then I was asked to line the staff up at the front entrance so the couple could thank each person in my team personally, even the in-house police. Each person was given a white envelope and a warm thank you.

Prime Minister Blair and your wife, I don't know where you are and what you are doing, but I hope you are living an amazing life.

This was certainly a time for me to continue making patches to sew onto the quilt of my life, by hosting other presidents from Asia, Europe and Australasia at the Presidential Guesthouse. Some of these were Prime Ministers John Howard of Australia, Jim Bolger of New Zealand and Tomiichi Murayama of Japan, and Chancellor Helmut Kohl of Germany. I even had a special guest from the Caribbean, whom I met under quite strange circumstances.

Have you ever noticed how the wildest things happen in the morning? This is why I like to wake up early – to give myself enough time to prepare for the unexpected and do what I need to do.

On this particular morning in 1998, I was under the impression that President Mandela and his Cabinet had gone down to Cape Town to attend Parliament. I knew it was a weekday, but, given the long hours we worked, the days of the week were meaningless. We had a few days off, so my team and I would start a bit later, allowing us to recharge our batteries and strengthen our spirits.

The sun was so amazing that morning. As I lay in my bed, the trees embraced my room, their beautiful purple earrings hanging from their branches. The array of birds enjoyed the shade and the smell of nature at her best. The cool breeze blowing over me made me feel even more lethargic; I was dreaming about how successful and great my boys were going to become, watching them get their degrees and play sports with grace yet success.

I heard a car.

A door slammed, and then there came the sound of voices. I jumped out of bed. There was no time for clothes; I ran down the stairs in my PJ pants and T-shirt, sped down the kitchen passages, turned into the main passage and, as I was running, looked in all the rooms to check for anything out of place. All I could see was dirty cups and saucers on the tables. This made no sense: before I put my head on my pillow, I would always ensure that the house was perfect – ready for a last-minute arrival.

I heard a noise at the front door. I jumped down from landing to landing, skipping the stairs. As I got to the door, with all my energy I opened it as quickly as I could. The bulky door tried to assist me, creaking.

I leapt through the opening. There, to my surprise, stood my security in a line; a small convoy, with a few of the bodyguards, stared at me as if I had just pulled a rabbit out of my butt during a stand-up performance.

'Brett, how are you?'

'Mr Reinders, good morning to you.'

'Sorry, it looks like we startled you.'

'Did I miss something?'

'No, not at all. We needed a place to have a quick meeting, so we asked the police unit to open up. Knowing that you always have everything ready, we did not want to hassle you.'

'I really don't mind.'

'I know you don't. This was really a last-minute decision.'

I was relieved to know what was going on, but I was a bit annoyed that I hadn't been notified – it was still my baby.

With all eyes still on me, as I stood there in my sexies – you know, PJs – I said, 'Mr Reinders, if I may ask, who had the meeting here?'

'How rude of me,' John started.

I was still startled, and my heart was racing, and I was dazed after what had just happened, as he continued, 'President Fidel

Castro, this is our guesthouse manager and chef, Brett Ladds.'

'Pleased to meet you,' the president replied.

'Thank you, President. I do apologise for how I look. Normally I am clothed.'

I could see that Castro was just as startled as the rest of us. He reached into his jacket, took out two cigars, and handed them to me: 'Thank you for the time at the guesthouse.'

'Thank *you*, President.'

The next thing, John opened the door of the host car, and the president got in. Off went the small convoy.

There I stood, with two cigars from Cuba, given to me by Fidel Castro, in my pyjamas, in front of the Presidential Guesthouse of South Africa.

Needless to say, when I came to my senses I took the police officers inside and explained that what had just happened would never happen again – the guesthouse was still my jurisdiction, and they should always alert me whenever visitors arrived.

THERE WERE SO MANY OTHER encounters that I could tell you about. But I am saving some of these magical experiences to tell you about in my recipe book, so that you, too, can cater for anyone, from friends and family to kings and queens.

10
The president's birthday

ALL THE STATE VISITS and dignitaries' personal visits to President Mandela aside, the guesthouse was busy all the time – each minister was entitled to host one function a year. One of these functions was a belated seventy-eighth birthday celebration for the president hosted by the ministers and their wives. Tracey and I were invited, but I was not able to attend as I was doing the catering. My wife – my beautiful, petite, blonde wife – was too shy to go without me.

I set up the Banquet Hall and contacted all my suppliers to ask them for the best of the best of everything I ordered. When I informed them who the function was for and who was hosting it, the produce and other items that arrived were more spectacular than ever. All their invoices said 'Happy Belated Birthday, President Mandela'; under each unit price was written 'A/O' and, in brackets, 'Our present to you'. (I prayed that the president knew how many people in the world loved him so much.) I contacted the suppliers and told them that the president would never accept these gifts, as they were not allowed. One supplier after another said, 'Don't tell the president. It just an honour to be able to do it.'

Now *that* is love.

Even the flowers were sponsored: we had ginormous bouquets of brilliant white lilies on each table. The Banquet Hall looked like a fairy tale. I made a banner for the entrance for all to enjoy, and placed a large ice bucket there with Pêche Royale in it for the president – it was his favourite.

THE PRESIDENT'S BIRTHDAY

Before I carry on with the happenings of that day, let me tell you why President Mandela was never around for his birthday. He was too busy making the day special for everyone else. He would always put himself last and make sure everyone else was taken care of. I catered for a function that he hosted for about ten thousand veterans who had helped him and the ANC to come to power, for example. For years after he became president, he would still host this function to thank them for all they had done. He was one of the best-known men in the world, one who had suffered for his entire life before becoming president – yet, every year, he still made an effort to thank all who had helped him and the cause.

Oh, I have to say – I met Mrs Winnie Mandela for the first time at the veterans' function. After I had served the desserts, I was busy walking up and down the marquee walkways and checking up on all the president's guests. As I was making my way down to the far west end of the marquee, one of President Mandela's daughters came running up to me.

'Come, come! Come meet my mom!'

I was so bewildered – I had dealt with the whole family except a mom. As I was being dragged down the walkway, I saw Mrs Mandela standing there.

'Mom, this is the chef that we keep speaking about!'

I put out my hand to shake hers. Next thing, Mrs Mandela grabbed me and gave me the most beautiful love-hug I'd ever had. As she released me from her most comforting hug, the media asked for a photo. Before I knew it, I was swept off my feet and it felt as if Mrs Mandela was holding me in her arms.

After the media left, I gave Mrs Mandela a massive kiss on her cheek, took her hands in mine and told her that I had only read about her and had not known that she was so warm and loving. I thanked her for her family, and the fact that I was so accepted and loved. You see, now, how many patches there are on my quilt.

Got distracted there – now, back to President Mandela's birthday function.

After the day, most of the ministers left. Their wives had made a huge table and were enjoying the Hartenberg wines on the table. It was so beautiful to see. I asked to be excused as I wanted to fetch my wife from work, but promised to be back shortly. I collected her from the centre of town. As soon as we returned, some of the ministers' wives met us at the door.

'Tracey, come, we have a surprise for you!'

They ripped her out of my hands and dragged her into the Banquet Hall foyer. She had a look on her face from a long day at work. I followed them, curious to see what was going on.

As soon as the other wives in the Banquet Hall saw Tracey in the foyer, they got really excited. One of them jumped up and gave a thumbs-up towards the stage. As they pulled Tracey into the Banquet Hall, I peered inside. There on the stage was the famous singer who had performed for the president earlier. I recognised her from the first time I'd seen her when she'd arrived that morning. She stood there in a long, sleek, black dress, a beaded band around her head. Alone on the stage, she held the microphone stand like an angel holding a wand.

Everyone in the Banquet Hall fell silent.

Miriam Makeba looked up as she started singing 'The Click Song'. As her voice travelled around the hall, you could see her notes, the wings of all the beautiful, gliding, bright-coloured swallows dipping and turning in the air above us. Her voice was the sound of rain breaking a drought, soothing all it touched. In the passion in her voice as she sang, you could almost hear the millions of voices who celebrated the end of the struggle and the days of victory ahead.

Everyone tried to soak up all the energy and passion we were feeling, our minds recording this experience in slow motion, ensuring that we didn't miss a thing and would be able to play back this honour over and over in our heads for the rest of our lives.

When Miriam stopped singing, our postures collapsed; you could see our bodies yearning for more of that soul from her voice. When she looked at us, we broke into a frenzy – not for the high of the music, but of thanks for what she had just given us. We whistled and clapped and shouted our thanks for the present we would carry with us forever.

Miriam came over and met my wife, then I thanked her for what she had done for her. As one would expect from all the most beautiful, powerful people I had met in my time at the guesthouse, Miriam, too, was humble and kind. She sang her praises to the ministers' wives and said it was her honour to have done it.

She smiled at me, and took my hand in hers: 'Just know one thing. From what I have heard today, you mean a lot to these people.'

I thanked her again and hugged her as if I were a son going off to war and she was my mom.

I left my wife with the ministers' wives as she was more comfortable now, and had met them at the Cabinet braais and around the estate. I went to join my team. We cleaned up and packed everything we'd used for the beautiful celebration away.

Later, my wife came to the scullery. I could see she was a bit pickled – not like sweet-and-extra-sour cucumber, just lightly pickled in sugar water. I took her upstairs and went back down to finish cleaning the Banquet Hall.

After each function or state visit, the guests would take the flowers home with them. This time, they'd all been left on the tables. I called my two drivers. We collected all the flowers and the drivers started dropping them off at the houses where the ministers were staying on the estate.

The last house they got to was Deputy Minister Pahad's. The drivers never knew how many ministers were around, so they had given each house only one bouquet. By the time they got to Minister Pahad's house, there were about six bouquets left. When they were let in to the minister's house, they took all the flowers inside and put them in various places around the house. They returned, and we completed our tasks. I sent the team home, and went upstairs to have a bath.

When I was ready, I went outside to join my wife on the Banquet Hall roof for a nightcap. My phone started ringing in the kitchen. I jumped up and hurdled through the window. As I got to it, it stopped ringing. So, I phoned the number back.

'Chef, this is Aziz Pahad.'

'Evening, Minister. Sorry I missed your call. How can I help you?'

'Yes … someone died.'

'Sorry, Minister?'

'It looks like someone died.'

'Must I phone the control room?' I said, alarmed.

'No, Chef. My house looks like a funeral home. There are flowers everywhere.'

'Sorry about that, Minister.'

'No, thank *you* – just, next time, one or two will be fine.'

'Sorry again, Minister. Have a great evening.'

I put down the phone and went back to my wife outside, where we lay against the skylights looking at the Milky Way. We were in tune; I could feel our thoughts thanking God for our experiences, the people we had met and how blessed we were.

11
Africa comes south

In my years at the guesthouse, I hosted and cheffed for several presidents from Africa. Among them were the presidents of Namibia, Rwanda, Botswana and Angola. The more memorable visits were from Zimbabwe's President Robert Mugabe, Swaziland's King Mswati III, Ghana's President Jerry Rawlings, Côte d'Ivoire's President Aimé Henri Konan Bédié, and the Democratic Republic of Congo's President Laurent-Désiré Kabila.

Please, I ask readers to remember that I am not political, nor do I pass judgement on what people do in the political world. But when I saw that the next state visit was Robert Mugabe from Zimbabwe, I was not impressed and did not look forward to hosting him. It had nothing to do with politics; it had everything to do with the way he treated people and how many people had died because of the way he ran his country.

When we started meeting the embassy delegation in August 1994, I could see that the delegates had more fear about everything being perfect than excitement that their president was coming to South Africa. Most of the meetings were about how not to upset President Mugabe, and what to do to impress him. In one of the final meetings before the state visit, I was told that I had better be one of the best chefs to impress President Mugabe and that it would be better if one of my maître d's dealt with him.

That was it for me. I had nothing against the delegation – they were good people, open and friendly and very easy to deal with. But all their actions and words were based on fear. I told them that, if I could please President Mandela and his Cabinet, and that I'd been entrusted with looking after, catering for and hosting all President Mandela's guests, I was sure that President Robert Mugabe would be pleased. I also told them that I would look after each guest in person, and would not hide who and what I was. To this, John Reinders replied with a smirk; Mary just turned around and said, 'Chef, you tell them.'

They started to apologise to us, saying that they were just advising us. Mary made it very clear that this was South Africa, and that people who came here were guests of South Africa and were expected to enjoy our hospitality, not question it. You go, Mary.

The day of the state visit arrived. Everything was ready in the guesthouse – no matter who the guests were, they had been invited by my president, so I made sure that everything was perfect and that my name and reputation would continue to fly high.

When President Mugabe arrived, I greeted him and offered to escort him to his suite to freshen up. Being human, I automatically disliked him; after all the advice about how to treat him, I really did not want him there. He did not say much as we walked. I assumed he was too scared to speak and sound like the moron that I thought he was. When I gave him the tour of his suite, it felt like his eyes were judging me and hating every second of me.

I was just leaving his suite when he called me back in and started speaking to me. Crap, crap, crap – he was so well spoken, he spoke with such sincerity, and he was so kind. He actually sounded caring. When I'd left his suite and assisted all his ministers into their suites, I went downstairs and poured a glass of wine. I was confused – I felt like a coelacanth on a beach, not knowing whether I should be in or out of the water.

Later that evening, after I had fed the whole delegation, I got a message that there was a car coming up to the guesthouse. I went downstairs to await the visitors, the president's head of security standing with me. A car stopped, with no security or bodyguards. Four white men stepped out. They shook my hand, but hugged the security guy, so I assumed they all knew one another well.

I asked if I could escort them upstairs and was told not to worry. I sent the team to go and rest – I did not want them waiting around for only four guys – and sat down in a wingback chair in the passage. I must have dozed off; when I heard a door open I jumped up and it was a few hours later. The men left; I saw the same routine every night.

Every time I dealt with President Mugabe, he was extremely friendly to me and greeted me by name. There was not a meal I served that he did not thank me for, and he never, ever moaned about a thing. He was an absolute pleasure.

Through my experience with President Mugabe, I saw only a wise man who cared for everyone, even if you were white. None of my team felt intimidated or threatened. I am not telling you this to condone what he did, but he was amazing to me.

There are all kinds of people in the world.

I WAS STANDING OUTSIDE THE GUESTHOUSE in March 1996 waiting for Swaziland's King Mswati III, even though I knew his plane had not landed yet. Everything was ready: the team, the food, the flowers – we were really just standing outside because the king was that late and we had nothing else to do. Foreign Affairs minister Alfred Nzo stood in the shade of the porte-cochère, just as bored as we were.

The whole time, at the guesthouse, we were listening to the radio.

'Stand by, here comes a plane.'

The plane would land and taxi in close to where the convoy was standing.

'False alarm. This is not the king's plane.'

We depended on this communication from the air force base at

Waterkloof. We would all sigh, then wait for the next radio alert, praying that the next plane would be the one.

Eventually, one of my in-house security detail could not handle it any longer. After the next false radio transmission, he grabbed his radio, strode out into the middle of the driveway, and looked up at the sky as if he was speaking to someone up there: 'Look for the fucken roof rack on the airplane. If there is no roof rack, don't radio in, fuck it.' He turned around and walked straight back inside into the security room, lay down on the couch, put his cap over his eyes, and looked like he was taking a siesta.

The radio was dead quiet for quite a while after that. The minister looked up at the trees and the guesthouse roof as if he had not heard the outburst, but I could see that he'd enjoyed it.

After quite a while, we got the next radio transmission, stating that the convoy was turning into Church Street. The next thing I knew, the convoy was hurtling up for the king to come and enjoy our hospitality.

Eddie Meiring got out of the car, as he always did, gave the signal, all the bodyguards got out, and then the king stepped out. If ever there was an African Thor, King Mswati III was it – young, well-built and good-looking. Look, I bat and don't bowl. I am straight and love women. Many a time I've joked with my wife and said I wished I was bisexual so that, when I walked into a nightclub, I'd have a one hundred per cent chance, instead of a fifty per cent chance. Needless to say, I have a fifty per cent chance – but hell, this was a stud muffin. As I walked him up the stairs, he asked whether I gymed. I told him I did, and all we spoke about after that was gym and how much weight we pushed on which machine. The only thing we didn't do was fist-bump each other and do a victory dance.

I did the tour of his suite, took all his dignitaries to their suites, and went downstairs.

One of King Mswati III's bodyguards was a real pain. He

thought he was in charge. Every time there was media around, or someone with rank, he made a scene or tried to get noticed. When I got downstairs, he was at the front door, causing a scene about the security man's comment about the king's plane. Not sure why – there was no media around. After giving a lllloooooonnnnggggg lecture, he demanded to know who had made the comment. I believe Minister Nzo was just as tired as the security detail of hearing the royal bodyguard's voice.

Swaziland's King Mswati III (centre) and I found we shared an interest in working out.

'Excuse me,' he said, 'we are having a meeting in the lounge. What is this all about?'

'Sorry, Minister. Something was said on the radio and I want to get to the bottom of it.'

'Listen to me, I was standing outside the guesthouse the whole time and nothing was said from this side. Now, take this elsewhere.'

The minister went back to the lounge. I called our security upstairs to the kitchen for a 'meeting', and told the visiting bodyguards to get out of the guesthouse. I think they were so relieved. When we all got to the kitchen and looked at one another, we started rolling on the floor with laughter. The comment had not been passed vindictively – it was made purely out of frustration, and this knobhead had come along and tried to make a big thing out of it.

I worked with King Mswati III throughout his visit and he was just so amazing. Even when he was dealing with President Mandela, he was true to himself and did not change character at all. We spent a lot of time just talking, about life and the world we live in. I could not get over how humble he was about being a king. When I saw him on other occasions after the state visit, when he was on official business in South Africa, he would always make an effort to greet me – by my name, too. Obviously, we would first see who had put on weight and was not gyming hard enough, but the honour was all mine.

King Mswati III, I salute you, sir.

President Jerry Rawlings' July 1998 state visit was running like clockwork. I swear, he could have been President Mandela's brother. Now, in life, if someone says, 'It's my opinion,' you can't argue with them – it's their opinion, after all. All I am saying is that the two men were so similar in so many ways.

Like President Mandela, President Rawlings was charming, humble and caring. He listened to everyone and was sympathetic to all people's needs. But …

On the night of the state banquet, I contacted President Mandela's head of security to see how far away they were. As I did with Queen

Elizabeth, and at every state banquet, I would run up and down the stairs to inform the visiting dignitary how the timing was going.

I walked briskly to the Banquet Hall to inform Protocol about the timing of President Mandela's arrival, and approximately how long it would take for the two presidents to meet, walk down the passage, and enter the Banquet Hall. John Reinders told me that everything was ready, and that all the guests were present and expecting the presidents.

'President entering the main gate,' I heard on the radio. I did the final leg in my relay to make sure that both presidents got to the finish line at the same time, then shot down the stairs and stood at the main door, waiting for President Mandela. I felt like a matric waiting for his prom queen outside her house while the whole family is taking pictures.

I greeted President Mandela, as elated to see him as I always was. It always took a lot to hold myself back from hugging him. I assisted him up the stairs to the bottom of the landing where the wooden stairs meet the main passage. I looked up – there was no President Rawlings walking down the stairs with his wife, Nana Konadu Agyeman-Rawlings.

After a few minutes, President Mandela looked at me as if it were my fault – as if I had not done what was expected of me. So, I went up the stairs and asked President Rawlings' aide if they were ready. He informed me that they would be out shortly. I walked briskly down the stairs and informed President Mandela.

'Did you not inform President Rawlings that Tata was on his way?' Mary's words made me feel like I was being scolded.

I knew that I had done my job, kept the visiting president informed, checked with the Ghanaian protocol officer, and confirmed times with them earlier that afternoon. President Mandela started to look and become impatient, moving around slightly at the bottom of the stairs. I had noticed that he had taken longer to get up the stairs that night, and that he'd leant on me more than usual, so I assumed his knee was acting up. I could understand that he did not want to stay standing unnecessarily.

I went upstairs again and knocked on President Rawlings' door. 'President Rawlings, President Mandela is waiting for your company in the main passage.'

I tried to be polite and formal, but I am sure everyone could hear the stress in my voice. President Rawlings' aide came to me, quite annoyed, and informed me that I had just breached protocol. I explained to him that I had done what my president had asked me to do. This was a lie, but I needed to show President Rawlings the urgency of the situation.

When I started walking back down the stairs, and Mary and the president saw no President Rawlings behind me, President Mandela took a seat in one of the wingback chairs in the passage. This was no easy feat for him; as he sat down, I could see the discomfort in his face and how tightly his knee was bandaged through his trousers.

Mary took me aside where no one could hear us. 'Did you notify their protocol officer that everything was on time today?'

'Yes, Mary. After the banquet we can meet and confront him.'

'Did you give President Rawlings all the time alerts?'

'Mary, you've already asked me this and I've confirmed. I have been up and down those stairs like a jackrabbit. I even knocked on the door myself. Really, Mary, this is out of my control.'

'Well then, Chef, it's my turn to go upstairs.'

As Mary went to the lift and pushed the button, I heard movement upstairs. 'Wait, Mary – I think they are coming.'

We went down the passage to the president, who was still sitting in the chair. Mary went to him as I climbed the stairs. Halfway up, I saw President Rawlings and his wife walking down the passage. I quickly went downstairs and told President Mandela that they were on their way; he stood up slowly, trying to mask the pain, then walked to the entrance of the stairwell and waited. We could now hear them coming down the stairs.

I saw the First Lady of Ghana first. She looked breathtaking – so beautiful, a true image of how beautiful women are in Africa. Just behind her was President Rawlings, looking as dashing as a president should. You could see their faces light up as they saw President Mandela.

As they were about to take the last few steps, President Mandela stepped forward and looked President Rawlings straight in the eye: 'President, I am not sure how important punctuality is in your country and if time matters there, but here in South Africa punctuality is important. I would never keep another president waiting for me, out of respect.'

Oh my soul, I thought, *did that just happen?*

'I do apologise, President Mandela. My wife was just taking time, as a woman normally does.'

President Mandela turned and stood to one side as the first lady came down. He complimented her on how beautiful she looked, and started walking her down the passage towards the Banquet Hall with President Rawlings behind them.

Everyone at the main table chatted and seemed to get along well that night, despite the incident. I was just so impressed with my president, who took no nonsense from anyone. I must say, that night opened my eyes.

While I fed the bodyguards, we all did what we usually did during the speeches: sit around and share a great laugh, no Russians this time. The bodyguards informed me that President Mandela had decided to take a few days off. He was the boss, so he could do as he pleased. I saw a gap and decided that I, too, would go down to my holiday house on the coast near what used to be the Transkei. While we were speaking, I asked which route they took back from dropping the president off, also in the Transkei. I realised that they would be driving right past the area where my holiday house was.

It is human nature to forget the bad. Think about it – when you break up with a girlfriend or boyfriend, months later you question your decision and only remember the great times. The bad times float away like the scorpion down the river. So, I invited them to stay over for a day or two. We all started making plans – as always, the best part of going on holiday is the planning.

I went down to the coast with my family and rested. Then, it was time to party – a day or two later, the bodyguards phoned to say that they had just dropped off the president and were on their way. When they arrived, there were a lot more guys than usual. Normally, they would only drive down with the required team, but this time, all of them had had to accompany the president.

We started off by trying to impress one another. All the war stories started coming out. Later that afternoon, we ended up at a bar called Pistols, a local hangout that was extremely vibey. We saw a poster advertising a beach party in Margate the following night, with top bands and DJs. Immediately, the bodyguards all asked if they could stay a day or two longer. Obviously, given the awesome time we were having, I said yes, no problem.

The following morning started as usual – beers on the beach, followed by sports on the beach. That afternoon, we went home and got ready for the beach party.

We arrived, and started in the big league – drinking, dancing and partying like hooligans.

The guys soon started wondering how they could impress the crowd and make a bigger bang than the bands and the DJs. They were arguing and agreeing at the same time. Then, the smallest of the bodyguards – who was in charge of the technical side of things – said, 'Let's shake this beach and stun this place.'

I looked around. There were more than twenty thousand people enjoying the party. They all started high-fiving each other, looking like naughty little boys who had just learnt to wee and were peeing into the pool together.

'Chef, we bet you all the drinks tonight that we can silence this whole place for a minute tonight – like in the next twenty minutes.'

Before I could disagree and start begging them to think their plan through (even though I didn't know what their plan was), they disappeared into the crowd.

I tried to find high ground so I could see where they had gone. *If anything goes wrong*, I thought, *I am grabbing my wife, jumping in our car* (I was wise enough to have brought my car), *and racing back to our house to deny everything.*

'Look, look, there they are,' said my wife, slightly nervously.

'I decided to run down to the beach, but the next moment there was a deafening blast, followed by the sand shaking like a dog that has just been sprayed down with water. My ears instantly started ringing, as if I were the clapper in a church bell. Then came this fine mist of seawater that fell like a blanket trying to silence all of us – a two-second rainfall that drenched everyone within thirty metres of the incident.

I stood up and started staggering to the shoreline, looking as drunk as a hobo who had found a hundred bucks in the street.

They certainly won the bet: as I staggered down, I imagined I could hear people's hearts beating in their chests. In the distance there was a faint whine; the closer I got to the shoreline, the louder the whine became, until I realised it was a siren.

'What the fuck did you guys do?'

They pushed right past me as if they did not know me, their badges in their hands, shouting to the people close to the shoreline, 'Move back! NIA! We are in charge – move back here!'

As their first line of defence went by, like the tacklers in American football, the next wave came, with the quarterbacks and backs collecting any evidence of shrapnel that had been left behind.

'Chef, you see, we told you. The whole beach shook and there was a minute of silence,' they said as three of them chest-bumped one another with pride.

In the time it took for a few waves to wash ashore, the police were there. The entertainment stage was still silent, like my son's room when he tries to sneak out to see his girlfriend. There were flashlights all over the place, with police shouting questions about what had just happened and whether anyone had seen anything. They started heading our way. When they reached us, the bodyguards showed their badges to the police and started reassuring them that they had everything under control. If you think about it, they did outrank any person on the beach. As they were all Special Forces, the police were overawed – and relieved, at the same time, to have backup of that calibre for an incident of this nature.

'Station Commander, look here – casing of a hand grenade.'

One bodyguard leapt over all of us and instructed the police officer to put the grenade down. 'What are you doing? This has now turned into a terrorist attack and your prints are all over it, Commander. Instruct your people to back off! This has now escalated far beyond your pay grade!' He said this with such authority and was so convincing that I almost believed him. 'Why are you guys just standing there? Go fetch the evidence kit from the cars!'

The two bodyguards next to me bolted up the beach and returned with a black bag.

'Stand back!' they said, using their size and strength to push the police, and bystanders, back. 'Turn off your torches! We need to use our infrared goggles to look for any more explosive materials!'

The police got so in the zone that they switched off their torches and started running around, killing any lights they could.

The bodyguards formed a ring around the hand grenade. I stood where I was – I had to see what was going on. The small bodyguard bent down, took his sunglasses out of the black bag, and put them on.

Immediately, I knew that this was bullshit. The next thing, he opened the bag a bit more. As he scratched around in it, I saw his dirty scants and the shirt he had worn yesterday. No wonder the bodyguards had made a circle and turned off all the lights. He took out a pair of long-nosed pliers, picked up the grenade, and placed in a plastic bag from a local shop. *Fuck, really?* I thought.

He put everything back into the black bag with his dirty scants, took his sunglasses off, and placed them in his pocket. He picked up the bag as if it were a trip switch that would set an atomic bomb off if not held level and carried as if his life depended on it, with the station commander and his police clearing the way. As he moved up the beach, I just stood there. Before I knew it, I was wet – I'd been tackled into the waves by the other bodyguards, who thought this was hilarious. I really should have known; I was an ass.

At the time I was not amused, though, so I stood up and walked up the beach, drenched. Just before I got to my wife, I saw the bodyguard and the police at President Mandela's convoy cars, all these executive cars with their police lights. I heard the bodyguards tell the station commander to go and write up a report about the incident, with witnesses' accounts if there were any, and that they would contact him in the week for the full report to present it to the minister.

I turned and went to my wife, to look for a dry shirt and a towel. Needless to say, I got a tongue-lashing from her as I had left her there and had not been around to protect her. I started to explain what had happened, that the bodyguards had caused the whole thing.

I got a clip on the head from my wife: 'Do you think I am stupid? Of course it was them! I want you to protect me from their stupidity!'

Within ten minutes they were all with us again, laughing, celebrating their victory and ripping the shit out of the police and how they had handled it.

Once I'd had a drink or two and my wife had told me to lighten up (after *she* had freaked out, remember?), I started to see the funny side.

We had an awesome night from then on. We drank, we danced and we lived.

Of course, I went home poor – I had to pay for the whole night's drinks.

When President Bédié and his delegation arrived in September 1998, I settled him and the delegates in and went back downstairs to the kitchen to start preparing the day's meals and snacks. I'd done research about the country, as I did for everyone who visited, to do all I could to make them feel at home, yet still experience South African culture and food.

I was busy doing preparation when a member of the embassy party walked up to me with three gentlemen. He introduced them to me as President Bédié's chefs, and told me that they would like to cook a meal for President Mandela on one of the nights of their visit. I had no objections, and let them know that they needed to clear this through the Protocol office. I gave them John Reinders' contact details.

When the chefs arrived, they brought three brown suitcases with them and placed them in the kitchen. I didn't really take notice of them until we were cleaning up that night and mopping the floors. I went to talk to the gentlemen about them. They were sitting outside in the quad enjoying my food.

I first tried speaking English, asking them off the bat what was in the suitcases and whether we needed to lock them away or put anything in the fridge or freezer. We all expect, when we are in our own country, that everyone can speak our language, but the men frowned at me. As they chatted among themselves, I could see that they were as confused as I was.

I gestured for them to come to the kitchen. As we got there, thank goodness, one of the president's aides was on his way in. I asked him to ask the chefs about the suitcases.

The aide assured me that the suitcases could be left where they were, so I did as they requested. I assisted the aide with milk and some tea, and then went upstairs for a two-hour power nap before the next day began.

After the first day, once of my chefs mentioned that there was a peculiar odour coming from the suitcases. As I got closer to the cases, I smelled what I would say was less of a smell than a warning that the food in the suitcases was in dire need of refrigeration. The visiting chefs had been looking over our shoulders the whole time. We'd tried to explain what we were doing during our prep, and they'd been extremely interested. Eventually, a member of the Department of Foreign Affairs' African desk came to the kitchen to ask a few questions. I jumped in before he had a chance to ask anything, and asked him to double-check whether the suitcases were fine there and that nothing could be going off inside them. He had a brief conversation with the chefs, and they exchanged a few laughs. He then walked up to me and tried to reassure me that everything was fine, and that they knew what they were doing.

The next few days continued as per the schedule. The only thing that changed was the odour from the suitcases: it went from suggesting to making a statement, and a gooey mixture started leaking out of them. On the day before the state banquet, Protocol informed me that the chefs would be making their traditional dish for President Mandela that night, who would meet President Bédié for a working dinner. I told the aide that it was protocol for me to make dinner too, even though everyone would be eating the dinner made by the visiting chefs.

They came to me with a list of ingredients, including fruit and vegetables, that they would require – all written in English, so I was sure it came from the embassy. I sent my chefs to fetch everything;

we remained on standby to assist the visiting chefs where we could, and I prepped the backup for dinner that night.

They cut the vegetables and spiced all their dishes, then placed a large pot on the stove and dropped a lot of whole vegetables into the water. This pot must have boiled for a few hours; all they did was keep topping up the pot with water. Once all their side dishes and starches were made (I must say, they tasted and looked totally amazing – I was dying to eat the leftovers), they fetched the suitcases and placed them on the stainless-steel tables right next to the stove. As if in a race, everyone in the kitchen gathered to see what was inside them. Even our protection detail stepped in to see.

As they opened the suitcases, I saw that each suitcase had a fish in it. The fish were smelly, sure, but did not honk as much as they should have, considering they'd stood in the kitchen unrefrigerated for that many days. They were whole, and had not been cleaned. Their eyes were still glassy and had a clear, sticky film over them, the same gooey stuff that had been leaking from the suitcases. I sent one of my chefs to fetch three trays that the visiting chefs could use to start prepping the fish, but before the chef had returned, the visiting chefs had poured the fish into the pot.

I stood back, thinking that they must know something I didn't. I just know that the spices and vegetables seemed to have blanketed the odour of the fish. My president was going to eat the food; I was going to ensure that whatever he ate was only the best, and I would not eat that fish.

I called the embassy spokesman to the kitchen about an hour before dinner and explained that President Mandela would be able to eat everything except the fish, as it was too spicy and the dish contained many vegetables that he was not allowed to eat. When the spokesman explained this to the chefs, they looked as sad as one could expect – they obviously wanted to add President Mandela's magical name to their CVs as someone for whom they had cooked.

This escalated to the African desk. John Reinders politely called me out of the kitchen and asked me what the whole storm in a teacup was about. After I'd explained the situation to him, he walked over to the pot and looked inside. I gestured to one of their chefs to let John taste the fish. As John looked up, he saw what I was doing; in a whisper, he told me that he would not taste the fish. I explained that this was a traditional dish from the Ivory Coast.

Needless to say, lamb was the main course that night. After that, any food served at the guesthouse besides mine had to be reported and placed on an official state visit document.

President Mandela never found out what happened that night. If he had, I bet my all that he would have eaten what he was served so that no one would have been disappointed.

People ask me how great President Mandela was. He was that great.

On the weekend, when the state visit was over and we'd all gone home to rest, the bodyguards invited me and the family to have a braai at one of the pools on the estate. I decided, this time, that a cold beer and great laughs were more important than rest. So, we joined the bodyguards and were having a grand time.

Now, as you can imagine, when twelve bodyguards who are larger than houses have a great time the alcohol runs out. They asked me whether they could buy from me through the guesthouse – that was not going to happen. As all the bottle stores were closed, I suggested that I phone a friend who had a bottle store in Silverton. We could maybe go there and buy from him, even though he was closed.

Silverton was not one of the best areas in Pretoria. It was at the other end of Church Street, far from the city centre. But one of the bodyguards at the braai had been a driver and bodyguard for one of the past presidents; as he still had that president's car, and was the junior in the crowd, the others told him to take me to Silverton to my friend's bottle store.

There we were, getting into the Mercedes-Benz in which the ex-president had been driven around – an extremely fast car – with a hulking, aggressive bodyguard (who had some drinks in him and was trying to impress me) behind the wheel.

Let me relate this parable. Two guys were walking across the street, chatting as they went. The next thing, one friend jerks his bud away, as if he was about to be hit by a car.

'Look what you almost stood in!'

They both bend down and smell it.

'Smells like crap,' they straighten up and agree.

They bend down again, and feel it. 'Feels like crap,' they straighten up again and agree.

They then bend down again, and taste it. 'Tastes like crap,' they straighten up and agree one more time.

As they walk past the crap, one looks at the other and says, 'Thank goodness we didn't step in it.'

That was the situation I was in. The driver was jumping traffic lights, knowing that the car was as good as a diplomatic passport. He was speeding and trying to act cool while gunning it. Sitting in the front seat, I turned from white to yellow to green to purple.

Eventually, we got to the bottle store and purchased the alcohol. The more I begged the bodyguard to drive nicely, and told him he was driving like a hooligan, the more he thought I was complimenting him.

We got back into the Mercedes-Benz, and it seemed that it had finally sunk into his macho head that I was begging, not praising. He slowed down to an acceptable speed and actually started stopping at red lights. We started talking, me asking him about things he'd experienced and people he'd protected and driven. The next thing, I was screeching like a cat that had just sat in spirits and run past a fire. I was pointing with all of me – hands, fingers and feet – at the hijacker who was pointing a gun at him and shouting. Well, I could see him shouting, but not hear him – as the shock kicked in, my ears shut down.

Out of nowhere, the bodyguard started shouting back. I wanted to kick him in the head to get him out of the car so the hijackers could take it, but by now I was so full of fear that my legs were numb. I was trying to call for help, but my lungs had decided to take more drastic action, refusing to breathe. That way, I am sure, they thought the hijacker would not shoot me as he'd think I was already dead.

Then, two cracks. It sounded like a car had hit us from behind and another car had hit that car. I looked to see if the bodyguard was okay and was amazed to see that he had just got even more upset. There were two marks on the window with cracks around them. I could not fathom whether I had been shot, or he had, or if we were both just in shock and didn't realise that we'd both been.

He just accelerated, did a U-turn and sped off.

'What are you doing?' I yelled.

'I am going to catch that bastard!'

'Are you hit?'

'No!'

'Am I hit?'

'No!'

'How do you know?'

'Shut up and help me look for him!'

'How do you know I have not been shot?'

'Bulletproof glass, Chef, no fucken way. Keep an eye on him!'

I could see the hijacker running. The bodyguard was trying to run him down. We were driving over pavements, over traffic islands, even down the wrong side of the road. Eventually, he ducked down an alley. As the bodyguard tried to get out the car, I grabbed him. That's when I put my foot down: 'Take me back. Now.'

On the drive back I tried to compose myself. I did make like I was looking down a side street, turning around and taking a sniff: I was convinced I'd shat myself. All he could do was rant and rave that the guy had got away.

When we arrived back at the party and my wife saw me, she ran – she could see that there was definitely something wrong with me. Before I had the opportunity to relate my traumatic and life-threating experience, the bodyguard was already telling everyone at the braai. Of course, they all thought it was hilarious.

That, I think, was scarier than having the bodyguards wake me in the middle of the night, or waking up hearing people shouting in the guesthouse. Come on, now – how much can my heart handle?

After that, I never went to a party with all the bodyguards at once. They are mad. Amazing guys, who have no fear and live life on the edge – but a bit too close to the edge for me.

In life, we have the opportunity to deal with all kinds of people, and President Laurent Kabila was one of the most unusual. I had dealt with kings, queens, presidents and celebrities. But a warlord? This was a first.

President Kabila arrived in July 1999 without any prearranged meetings and agendas. There were no formal bodyguards from the DRC. The convoy arrived and everybody got out. Behind the convoy were two cars filled to the brim with his security. I had dealt with bodyguards and security before, but never with security like this. They came across as stone-cold killers. Their faces had no expression. It looked like they had been placed on this earth just to fight.

When I escorted the president between his suite and the dining room, or to his meetings, I would speak to him to try to suss out the essence of this man. I had done my research; what I had read was that he was merciless and feared, and that ordering his troops to take lives did not concern him in the least. I had overheard some of the people from the Department of Foreign Affairs' African desk speak about him. They, too, said that he was one of the most feared men in Africa, and that life meant nothing to him.

Yet here I was, walking and speaking to him, like a groupie stalking a serial killer – you know, those crazy woolheads who sit in court galleries and shout 'I love you' to the serial killer on trial.

The powerful yet gentle President Laurent Kabila of the DRC.

I am sure everyone wonders what a killer looks like; we all know there is no distinctive look. The fact is that President Kabila was soft-spoken and kind. He was like a granddad, someone you just wanted to hug. I could see him sitting at the fireplace telling loving stories to his family and being Papa Bear, a cold killer behind the façade.

I was not surprised to learn that he was assassinated by one of his own bodyguards in 2001; I later met his son, Joseph Kabila, who succeeded him.

12
Rolls-Royces, cash and snipers

When Prince Sultan bin Abdulaziz Al Saud of Saudi Arabia came for a state visit in September 1997, I knew immediately after the first meeting that we were dealing with a different class of person.

In the meeting, his delegation laid down a list of requirements to be arranged and purchased prior to the sheik's arrival. For some reason or other, the Department of Foreign Affairs was not very accommodating; they were not interested in most of the requests and seemed to be quite hostile at times.

There was a really smooth man sitting in the meetings. He did not speak very much, and was not consulted about any of the decisions, yet I noticed him. Not because he had the most amazing smell about him. Not because he was dressed like his suits were made by a tailor. Not because he sat there with a sense of worth about him. I noticed him because every time he came for a meeting he was driving a different Rolls-Royce. So, even though he just sat there in the meetings, in some way he had power. I just could not place it.

A few days after the final meeting, I got a call from this gentleman requesting to come and see me. I asked whether I should arrange for representatives from Foreign Affairs to attend. He was not interested in dealing with them; he asked if he could see me alone, just to run through a few things. I had no objections, so I set up a meeting for the following day.

ROLLS-ROYCES, CASH AND SNIPERS

He arrived in a dark-blue Rolls-Royce that day. It was beautiful – as he parked, I just stood there drooling. Hell, they are beautiful pieces of art.

I was asked if we could do a final walk-through of the suites. He looked at me and told me that he required a lot more to be done before the visit. As I was explaining that I did not have the authority to use my budget for the requirements, he interrupted me: 'Why are you worried about money all the time? I tell you what I need, then you order it, and I will pay for it. Understand?'

I opened my notepad and had my pen ready.

In the main suite, for the sheik, he wanted eight televisions. Each television had to run its own channel – he handed me a list. Then, he gave me a list of blankets and bedding. As we walked around, he wanted furniture added, night blinds installed, and so on. Me being who I am, I told the smooth, rich gentleman not to worry – I would get everything done as requested.

My first call was to get the televisions set up. When I explained what I needed, the owner of the company wanted to come out and see the site. I asked for quotes for the bedding and the blankets, then started calling more and more companies to quote me on the items that needed purchasing and the jobs that needed doing immediately. The quote came through for the blankets: over R5 000 a blanket. This was at a time when bread cost R5.61 – it now costs R16.20 – so I imagine the blankets would cost over R15 000 today. And, he wanted twenty of them. Then the quote came through for the televisions and the satellite dish. It was nearly R100 000.

Once I'd got all the quotes, I contacted Mr Smoothie, who told me to go ahead. This made me nervous; I was calling in favours and placing orders without having the cash. The last thing I needed was to have this become my responsibility.

That night, I could not sleep. None of my suppliers had even asked for a deposit, and all the invoices were made out in my name.

I could buy a brand-new BMW with all the money that I owed on the invoices – all this for a four-day visit. I fell asleep eventually. What felt like moments later, I heard the wind outside laughing at me, knowing that what little sleep I'd managed to get was an illusion.

I went downstairs. The first call I got was from the guys who were on their way to install the satellite dish. They arrived in two bakkies: one full of televisions and the other with a satellite dish that was over three metres in diameter.

My phone rang. It was Mr Smoothie, wanting to know if I was in. I confirmed and phoned the gate to allow him in. He could not get there quickly enough. He gave me a brown paper bag with all the money neatly packed into it. I thanked him profusely. We shook hands and he was gone.

As the suppliers dropped off the stock or completed their jobs, I paid them. The blankets arrived. As I unwrapped them, I could feel why they were so expensive – they were like sex on naked skin, totally orgasmic.

On the morning of the sheik's arrival, Mr Smoothie came to check that everything had been done as requested. He walked around, then complimented me: 'I know who to rely on in life. It's a gift of mine. You are one of those people.'

I thanked him, and gave him a package containing the invoices and change. He handed it back to me: 'I don't need those. There was enough money, yes?'

'Yes, sir. There was too much – just over R9 000 too much.'

'Keep it for your efforts.'

'Sir, thank you, but no – I am not allowed to.'

'Come on, it's yours.'

'Thank you, sir.'

I knew the price of a new BMW as I had just bought one. This R9 000 would help nicely to pay it off.

'Sir, here are the invoices.'

'Please, I don't need them. If you don't want them, throw them away.'

These men are stupid rich. I am sure they weigh their money and don't count it.

I was not allowed into the suite when the sheik arrived. I could walk with him and speak to him until we reached the suite, then his own people took over. That's when I noticed how important Mr Smoothie was – he was walking in and out of the suite, telling everyone what to do and how to do it.

The delegation did not want dinner, as most of them were going out that night. From the ground floor we could smell their colognes and, man, they smelled great.

A little later Mr Smoothie came downstairs with a bank bag full of dollars and asked if I could convert them to rands – the guys who were going out needed cash for the night. I immediately phoned Lucas, the friend who had gone with me to Mamelodi the night of the shooting. His wife Leandri worked in the forex department of one of the big South African banks. I told her what I needed and begged her to assist me; she asked for a few minutes to get authorisation. During that time, I went to Mr Smoothie to ask him how much money was in the bag. He gave me the 'exact' amount: 'It's just under a bagful.'

'Sir, how much is that, please?'

'Chef, I don't know. I'm sure the bank will count it,' was the awesome response I got.

My phone started ringing. I excused myself and Leandri confirmed that she could assist me.

I jumped into a convoy car and a bodyguard raced me off to the city centre to do the exchange. I met Leandri at reception. She took me to the forex department; within twenty minutes, I'd been assisted and had the cash in three bags.

On the drive back – sirens on, hurtling through the traffic – the bodyguard asked, 'Chef, how much is in the bags?'

'Just over R436 000.'

'Chef, we could just keep driving.'

'I know, but that's not who we are.'

'You know I'm joking, Chef?'

'I know. I dream, too. Thank you for taking me.'

I got a wink and a smile.

When we arrived back at the guesthouse, I could smell Mr Smoothie in the lounge. I asked him to come with me to the office, where I gave him the bags. He turned them out on my desk, then took all the notes that had been bundled and packed them tightly into two bags. The R36 000 was lying loose on the desk.

'You can have the change, Chef.'

'Sir, that is a lot of money.'

'You can have it. I don't want the change.' He grabbed the two bags and walked out.

I was so excited I almost had sex with myself. I put the so-called change into the third bag and took it upstairs. So far, my two tips were half the value of my new car.

I was on form that whole visit. Not that I gave more, as I gave perfection every time – I just had such a happy tune playing in my head the whole time.

When the sheik had left and his state visit was being written in the history books, Mr Smoothie came back to the guesthouse and wanted to see me. I went down to meet him, feeling like we should use a secret handshake as we were brothers now. I greeted him; he asked if I still had all the invoices. I tried to keep my smile and the tune playing in my head, but like a tape that is stretched in a tape deck, it started going weird – into silence as the tape jams the deck. Had all this been too good to be true?

'Yes, sir. I did not throw the invoices away – I still have them.'

'They are in your name, and not the Department's?'

'Yes, sir. I had to put them in my name.'

ROLLS-ROYCES, CASH AND SNIPERS

'Perfect. Well, that is it from me. I wish to see you in the future and thank you once again for all you did for us. We will always be indebted to you.'

'What about the stuff?' I asked. 'The televisions, the blankets, all the stuff I had to buy – where should I send it?'

'It's yours, Chef. We don't need it. It's all yours – it says so on the invoices.'

He walked to his Rolls-Royce, climbed in, and was gone.

The tape had not jammed – it just needed to be turned around. I was jiving inside.

I got my team to go fetch everything that had been purchased, and shared it among them. I kept three blankets, though – I just had to sleep under a R5 000 blanket.

Now *that's* how a state visit should go. Amazing.

THE AMERICANS NEED TO HAVE their own section. They really know how to do things.

In February 1997, I hosted Vice President Al Gore's state visit From the very start, the Americans arrived punctually. They would all be dressed in suits. Even the women wore suit dresses, if that's what you call them. Prior to each meeting, we would receive a list of attendees, an agenda and a timeframe for each agenda item. I loved their professionalism and rigid outlook on meetings.

In the first – no, let me not lie, in the second – meeting, I was not paying very much attention to what was being discussed. I knew the minutes that would be sent out later would be on point and contain conclusions, not all the warra warra that builds up to the conclusions.

I was doing something different: I was drawing a seating plan on my notepad, writing down people's names. This took a while, as I would need them to say their name before they spoke. Then,

I looked at the way they were dressed and listened to what they were saying. Remember, in these meetings you discuss everything, no matter which department you are in.

First, I eliminated the South Africans. I knew that the lady on my right was from Public Works. Aside from the fact that she was trying everything she knew to break the chewing gum in her mouth and failing miserably, I'd had the unfortunate experience of dealing with her in the past.

Mary was on the opposite side of me. Obviously, I knew her. I loved that lady. She had her tea and honey next to her. Every now and then, she would wave tenderly to one of my waiters, and whisper something in his or her ear. The waiter would come back with some fresh fruit on a plate.

Sitting two away from me and two away from Mary must have been a new member of one of our departments. She was sitting and smiling as if the chair was vibrating. It looked like she knew how honoured she was to be sitting where she was. She had a large dhuku wrapped around her head. It looked like the material was from a shop where the salesman was better at sales than honesty. It was atrocious.

Eddie Meiring, my superhero, was to the left of Mary. Whenever he was around, I felt safe. Bring it on – I dare you, I have Super Eddie on my side.

Between me and the Queen of Sheba-material lady was a member of the Protocol department. She requires no introduction, having fallen on her ass in front of the Pope. Between Mary and the Queen of Sheba was definitely the head of their security. He had a smooth, bald head that was so well polished it shone. I could see bright little stars glittering on his head. He wore an earpiece connected to his walkie-talkie – only he knew who he was going to contact during the meeting. The best was that he kept his sunglasses on while he was indoors. Not even James Bond is that cool.

Next to Chappie Destroyer was a lovely little white lady with her hair all tied up. She sat there sweetly and looked kind. Definitely Protocol.

Drawing a seating plan was a way to entertain myself and to remember who was who.

Next to her was Bowling Ball Man, who I guessed was an embassy man. When he goes bowling, I am sure he never finishes a game without storming off. His friends would probably stick their fingers in his nose and their thumb in his ear and try to bowl him. If he did not have that smug look on his face, as if he knew everything and was better than everyone, and just smiled a bit, he could probably be a great man.

To his right was a beautiful, refined woman, very, very pretty and kind. She had greeted everyone and was really positive and optimistic. My guess was that she would be taking the minutes.

Mary called the meeting to order and introduced herself. She asked who was in charge representing the United States. Bowling Ball Man stood up and introduced himself – he was the ambassador, and said that he would be leading the meeting from the US side. As he sat down, he smiled and looked all of us in the eye and greeted us personally. He was an awesome man – friendly and happy. So, I got half a point for guessing that he was an embassy man, but no points for being a judge of character. He was amazing.

Mary introduced Eddie as our head of security and asked who was representing the US on the security side. I'd hit that one on the head: Bald Sparkly-head Man almost jumped to attention. Then he rambled some long rank that he had, with his authorisation class; Eddie stood up, shook his hand, and just said, 'Hi, I am Eddie.' I told you he was a legend. A full point for me.

The lovely, sweet lady was writing like mad. She would look up and smile all the time. Bowling Ball Man ensured that she was recording all the minutes, and asked her to get all our contact details to share after the meeting. Half a point for me.

Now I was dying to know what Hot Lady did. Where did she fit in? I leant over to Pope Lady and asked her who her counterpart was.

'In good time,' she said.

I begged her, said I had to know. She giggled at me: 'You're doing your game thing again, aren't you?'

Then: 'Excuse me, is there something you wanted to share with the group?' Mary looked unimpressed.

'Sorry, my lady. Yes, [Pope Lady] was just asking who was from the Protocol office.'

Pope Lady gave me such dirty look.

'I am sure she can ask herself,' Mary said. We felt like schoolkids being reprimanded by their teacher.

With a heavy Mississippi accent, the woman on her right stood up and introduced herself as head of Protocol. I did not see that one coming – I thought she was South African. I felt an obligation to take her to the nearest police station and make her open a case against the man who had sold her that fabric. I got no points for her.

So, I stood up and introduced myself. 'Stunning meeting you all. I am Brett Ladds. Everyone calls me Chef. I run the Presidential Guesthouse and am the executive chef.'

Mary jumped in. 'Chef is the only South African allowed upstairs. For the duration of your stay at the guesthouse, he will be your contact and go-between. Know that he is trusted – he is President Mandela's man.'

I stood there waiting for the pretty lady to say something. I had only stood up to finish my game, but she just sat there, silent.

'Sorry, my lady, who might you be, and from which department are you?'

She stood up and introduced herself. She was from Washington, representing the State Department from their African desk. Half a point for me.

Once all the meetings were done, which took about three weeks, it got down to logistics. I spent hours walking the Protocol people and security through the whole process, again and again. Then, they introduced different scenarios and possibilities. At that stage, I was irritated, but they were correct in their approach. I was taking notes, as they were teaching me a lot. Real notes.

After all the different run-throughs, we ended up in a meeting with security. You would think our security would have learnt from the Russians. The Americans were telling our security what they were going to be doing; our security was telling them that they had everything covered. It was like watching a married couple fight.

On the morning Vice President Al Gore was due to arrive, I was ready at 5 a.m. To the minute, the American security arrived and met with me. Their head of security, Bald Sparkly-head Man, instructed all the security to take their positions. As he was pointing the locations out, it was apparent that they had had numerous briefings – they knew exactly where to go. I counted fifteen snipers, and saw I don't know how many close combat security, as well as bodyguards.

These guys were organised, and ready for anything. They outnumbered all the security for all the previous state visits I'd hosted put together. They even had emergency helicopters at the embassy – I overheard this in a conversation.

When I went to the kitchen, I found that they had stationed a man at each door inside and around the kitchen. I contacted our security and Bald Sparkly-head Man, and explained that this was not happening – and that he could station all his security at the back door of the kitchen. Then he'd know that no one could come in – not even through the roof, as there was a sniper on the kitchen roof.

I said I wanted a list of all security in the house. I had the list of delegates, and there were a lot more people present than we had originally agreed upon. He excused himself and set a meeting for 'T minus twenty-five minutes' in the kitchen. I told Botes to wait in the kitchen. I gave him some food to taste and, as I carried on working, we had a chat about the visit.

At 'T minus zero minutes', he returned. In his hand he had four different pin badges. This shows you how organised they were: they had South African flags. He asked how many of our security were in the house. Botes showed him the list, and confirmed that the numbers and names were correct. Bald Sparkly-head Man then issued the correct number of badges to Botes. Then he showed us the other three, and explained what each badge represented: who was allowed in the guesthouse, who was allowed upstairs, and who was allowed everywhere.

Botes was happy, asked for one of each, then went to show them to his unit and explain them.

Bald Sparkly-head Man asked me how they would be able to identify me. I told him I'd be the guy welcoming the vice president at the front door and walking around the guesthouse making everything happen. I also told him that I had clearance for all areas. So, the best way to identify me would be my face. He did not find that funny at all. After all the meetings and briefings, I said, surely he could have informed everyone who the cookboy was. He then informed me that he would not take the blame if I got forcibly removed from an area. I asked him not to be hostile, but I should have realised that he had his nice face on. If I was removed, I said, he needed to understand that things would stop happening in the guesthouse, as I drove the machine. He looked me up and down and marched off.

I decided just to keep being myself and doing my job.

When the time came for the vice president to arrive, I took off my chef's jacket, put on my suit jacket and started making my way down to the front door. I was nervous. As I walked past each American security member, I looked at his security pin and greeted him with a friendly South African smile. I would get half a head tip, and their faces would follow me as I walked past – I could not see their eyes through their sunglasses.

I made it down to the front door without been forcibly removed from my own guesthouse. I went to greet Bald Sparkly-head Man by tapping him on the shoulder, then greeted all his security outside, smiling as I did so, hoping they would remember who I was while I was doing my job. I then went to check on our security to make sure they were ready.

The courtyard started filling up as more and more people began to arrive. I had to listen closely to our security radios to know what was going on; their security would just push on their earpieces and nod to one another.

Then the signal came that the vice president was entering the main gate. As in a war game, all the pieces took their places. The area under the porte-cochère at the front door was empty. I stood there with John Reinders. A few metres away, we were flanked by American security.

John welcomed the vice president and we started to walk into the guesthouse. As we got into the foyer, I was introduced. We went up the stairs to the lounge. I assisted the vice president with refreshments and ensured that he was comfortable.

I heard a disturbance at the main door. I promise you, it looked like a scene from Donkey Kong: all the security members were trying to get in, but Botes was standing in the middle of the doorway, grabbing them by their arms and looking at their badges. Those who had the right pins were pushed inside; those who had the wrong pins were flung back outside. Once Botes had decided that there was enough security in the guesthouse, he simply closed the door, locked it, took the key, and went to sit on his chair.

I wanted to run down and stop him – I was worried that it would become a problem at Foreign Affairs' American desk – but once Botes had sat down, Bald Sparkly-head Man walked up to him, checked whether he was happy, greeted him and went upstairs to the vice president. That was that.

The meetings went on throughout the all day. In between them, I fed the vice president without any problems, and fed all the security. Then the vice president left. Just like that, the snipers, close combat security and bodyguards evacuated. As quickly as it had started, it had all ended.

I locked up. With a stiff whisky, I sat for a moment, trying to make sense of these days.

13
Moonwalking with the stars

It wasn't all about heads of state during my time at the Presidential Guesthouse. During President Mandela's term, I had the honour of meeting, catering for and associating with many celebrities.

I catered for the 1995 World Cup Rugby champions, South Africa. They were incredible. I asked whether my brother could join me; we met with them and enjoyed the evening with them. I also catered for and hosted the African Cup of Nations winners, Bafana Bafana, in 1996. This was really a great event – as I walked around during the evening, I enjoyed the celebrations and camaraderie all around me. I am not a follower of soccer, so please excuse me – but South Africa were the champions, which is why I enjoyed it so much. I saw an old school friend at the event. We greeted each other as we embraced and I asked him what he was doing there. He told me that he played for Bafana Bafana. I knew he was good – just not that good! After a chat and a hug, I let him continue celebrating with his teammates.

As I passed the Minister of Sport and Recreation's table, Minister Tshwete asked me how I knew Mark Fish. I explained that we had been great friends at school, and asked him to excuse my ignorance.

Later, I walked past Mark on the way to fetch President Mandela, who had to depart. I shook his hand, and told him how proud of him I was and that I would always sing his praises.

THE MADIBA APPRECIATION CLUB

In 1997, a visit was arranged for Naomi Campbell and Quincy Jones to come and meet President Mandela. I had been a big fan of Quincy Jones since my school days – he was, and still is, one of my ultimate legends.

The first to arrive was Naomi Campbell. No large delegation or convoy escorted her – she arrived in an upmarket sedan. The door closest to me opened, and out climbed a tall, beautiful woman. She was *so* beautiful – naturally beautiful. As she climbed out and stood in front of me, I saw that she was a head taller than me. *Wow*, I thought. *This is hot.*

'Welcome to South Africa and to the Presidential Guesthouse, Miss Campbell,' I announced, as I tried to take her hand.

The next thing, Miss Campbell started acting as if she had a cramp in her neck from her long flight, her head gesturing at the car.

'Miss Campbell, are you fine?' I asked,

She leant in to me. 'Miss Campbell is on the other side of the car. I am her aide.'

As I tried to apologise, she nudged me to run and meet Miss Campbell. The woman who got out of the other side of the car did not look very impressed to be there.

'Welcome to South Africa and to the Presidential Guesthouse, Miss Campbell.'

'Where is my room?'

'Please follow me, Miss Campbell. I will escort you.'

'Bring my things,' she said to her aide.

I walked in front of her up the first stairs, then down the passage to the next flight of stairs that led to the top floor where the suites were.

'How many more stairs?'

'We are almost there, Miss Campbell.'

I could not wait to get to her suite so I no longer had to deal with her. I did the tour and asked if there was anything else I could get her.

'If I need anything I will send my aide.'

In all the state visits of all the high-profile people who'd had the honour of being invited by President Mandela to stay at the Presidential Guesthouse, I had never been treated so badly.

I went downstairs to fetch the beautiful aide and show her the way to her suite. As they were taking the bags out of the car, I asked the bodyguard why he had driven the wrong way around the circle – the guest's car door always faces the guesthouse door when the car parks under the porte-cochère. He said he hadn't thought about it, and realised what a grave mistake he'd made. We were all a bit embarrassed. Luckily, Miss Campbell had been speaking to him when I'd greeted the aide, and hadn't heard what transpired outside. The aide was just as relieved.

I took her upstairs to the suite right next to Miss Campbell's and went downstairs. The poor beautiful woman had to run up and down the stairs to fetch this and then that – I was not allowed to help or send any of my maître d's.

Later that afternoon, Quincy Jones arrived. I was so excited to meet him. He was just as cool and mind-blowing as I had expected. When he arrived, he did not want to go straight up to his suite. I took him to the lounge and gave him refreshments, and we stood around talking. I had to tell him what a huge fan I was, and for how long I had been following him.

He loved that I knew so much about him and had followed his whole career. But he was more interested in President Mandela and who had stayed in the guesthouse and the stories about our beautiful country. I informed him that Miss Campbell had arrived earlier, that she was upstairs, and that his suite would be on the other side of the house. He was just so awesome. He had no worries or concerns about anything.

I stood back as he took a seat after our chat, and looked at the master – the incredible Mr Quincy Jones was in the house.

I left the two parties to enjoy the house and the gardens. I had placed all my key people around so that no one would want for anything. I then went to both parties and invited them for dinner at 7 p.m. in the main dining room. I had prepared about three different meals in each course to ensure that you-know-who had nothing to moan about.

Supermodel Naomi Campbell was a demanding guest, but we developed a good rapport.

When I went upstairs to go fetch Miss Campbell for dinner, she looked a lot better. The aide turned to me and asked whether I would like to have a photograph with Miss Campbell. I thought it would be great to have. So, the photo was taken where we stood. You can see the happiness and joy beaming out of Miss Campbell.

At least one of us had a beaming smile.

Once they were seated in the dining room, and had started making conversation, I explained the menu and took the orders.

I went to my kitchen and started making all the meals. I really wanted to impress Mr Jones. He had been so patient and giving that I wanted him to feel like a king.

I sent the team in to serve the starters, and continued to make the main course.

When I saw the clean plates come out of the dining room, I knew I had nailed that course. Then a maître' d came to me to tell me that I was wanted in the dining room. *Fuck,* I thought. What could the problem be? If it was minor, one of my team could have handled it.

I walked into the dining room, still wearing my chef's jacket. 'Are you happy with your starters? How may I be of assistance?'

Meeting the great Quincy Jones (raising glass) was a real highlight for me.

Mr Jones – Mr Quincy Jones – stood up and started serenading my food. He started singing one of his songs as I tried to fight back the tears of joy. I was taken. Now I know how a woman feels when a man goes down on one knee and asks for her hand in marriage. I lie – it feels better than that.

I could not stop thanking him, then went back to the kitchen to cook the mains. After desserts, coffee and truffles, everyone went to their suites for the night as the following day they were meeting President Mandela.

Later, after I had finishing cleaning the kitchen and my wife was sitting at her usual spot – the plate warmer – while we had a nightcap, I heard a voice.

'Hello …'

It got louder: 'Hellooooo!'

My wife jumped up, as I was on the far side of the kitchen, at the pot sink. She stuck her head around the corner. I heard a finger click, then saw my wife get back onto the plate warmer and she continued speaking to me.

'My girl,' I said to her, 'is there someone there?'

'Yes,' she said.

'Please can you help them? Or are they gone?'

'No, they are just standing there.'

I wiped my hands with haste and threw the dishcloth behind me as I rushed out of the kitchen. It was Naomi, wanting tea before she went to bed. I obliged, prepared her tea and took it up to her room. When I got back, I asked my wife why she hadn't helped Miss Campbell – she could at least have assisted me.

'Have I *ever* not helped you?' my wife asked, annoyed.

'That's why I can't understand why you didn't help me now. That was Naomi.'

'I really don't care who it was. No one clicks their fingers to call me. Do I look like a dog?'

The following day was not a bright-and-early start, as we only served breakfast at 9 a.m. The two parties wanted to go shopping and do some touring in our capital – they were seeing the president later that afternoon, so there was time to kill. We cleaned the guesthouse and got everything ready for the arrival of the president.

When Mr Jones came back, he could not stop speaking about how beautiful our city is and how much he enjoyed the outing. A while later, Miss Campbell came back. We fetched her shopping and took it to her suite. She went and joined Mr Jones in the lounge for refreshments, then they went upstairs to get ready to meet the president of presidents.

Later that afternoon, I went to the suites and informed the guests that the president would be arriving in fifteen minutes. I made sure that all my team members were ready. On the way back to main door to welcome the president, I popped my head into the lounge to ensure that the celebrities were standing and waiting for him, in much the same way as their fans would wait to see them. I fetched the president at the front door. On the way up the stairs, he confirmed who was in the lounge and asked how things had been going. He, too, looked excited to see his guests.

As he walked into the lounge, Miss Campbell almost convulsed as she rushed to get to the president first. She could not stop saying that President Mandela was her father and she was his daughter. Then, the president greeted Quincy Jones. As they stood speaking, it looked as if they were long-lost friends. The president greeted everyone in the lounge, treating the aides and celebrity entourage with as much respect as the celebrities themselves. He was amazing, as always, and made each person in the lounge feel as if they were honoured guests.

Once the hype was over, I started serving refreshments and doing my duties. As I walked past the president, who was speaking to Naomi, he took my arm and gently drew me closer. 'My chef has been looking after you, Naomi?'

'Yes, thank you – he has been treating all of us very well.'

'Good. Chef and I have come a long way together, and all of us at the ANC have respect for him. Do you know that we used to live together here?'

I thanked the president as he continued speaking to Naomi – about me, I could hear.

After the meet and greet, the president departed, as they would all be seeing one another later. I walked him out and started heading back to the kitchen. I heard someone calling me. I knew who it was, but chose to ignore her for a bit. If there is one thing the president has taught me, it is to respect everyone, which I do – yet I feel that, if you have been disrespected after you have shown all respect, you change the game.

'Chef! Oh, Chef!' I heard, in the sweetest voice, which followed me to the kitchen. As I was about to enter the kitchen, I turned to her: '*So* sorry. I was *so* deep in thought.'

She spoke to me for a while, then gave me a butterfly wave as she turned to leave. For the rest of her stay, I was treated like *I* was the celebrity – I was greeted all the time, thanked and praised for everything.

Mr Jones did it from the heart; others did it because, all of a sudden, they realised I, too, knew the president. But, no matter what happened, after our celebrity guests had left I always felt privileged to have hosted and catered for them.

While I never had the honour of cooking for or hosting Luciano Pavarotti in person, I did organise a cocktail event in 1999 at which the president and his guests met him.

I did the evening cocktails and all the catering that was required. I met Luciano when he arrived at the function; once again, my hero president called me over while he was speaking to Luciano and introduced me to this legend of a man.

I don't appreciate opera, as millions of people do, but I do excuse myself as it is not for everyone. This did not take away my excitement about meeting and talking to Luciano Pavarotti, though. I appreciate success in anyone, and here was a giant of a man who truly came across as humble – a man who knew how blessed he was with his talent, and who really appreciated the fact that he could share his gift with so many.

If only I could have hosted him at the guesthouse, spent more time with him, and allowed some of his greatness soak into me. Thank you, Luciano Pavarotti. May your voice soothe the angels and fill the skies.

No matter who we are, or how old we are, we have all put on one glove, tried to do the moonwalk and grabbed our crotch – even if we were alone in the bathroom.

Michael Jackson had been my life's inspiration. His words had given me the power to get through puberty and dating. White socks and Chinese slippers? I'd worn them. Prince was my wife's field of energy, the one who'd inspired her from her childhood into adulthood. For my friend Drugs, it had been any band that made a noise with no rhythm. But Michael Jackson was my all.

When I heard that he was coming to meet the president, I jumped straight into my Kombi and raced to the Department of Foreign Affairs to see who was organising the visit. I *had* to be part of this, even if I only saw him walking past me. Mary thought I was very funny. With all the high-profile people I hosted, I would act like a child begging his parents to point out the Easter eggs in the garden. She had a good laugh, and told me that the Presidency was organising the visit.

I time-travelled in my Green Machine Kombi to the Union Buildings. I could hardly wait to park and get to John Reinders' office. Needless to say, I was singing 'Billy Jean' and 'Beat It' all the way.

As I went around each corner in the Union Buildings, I'd do a Michael Jackson spin. If there was no one around, I would grab my crotch.

I got to John's office and knocked as if I had to get in before the Grim Reaper got me. He opened the door and looked at me as if he'd just seen his mother naked for the first time.

'This is a first, Chef. What brings you here?'

'Mr Reinders, are you busy? May I have some of your time, please?'

'Sure. Come in.'

'Mr Reinders, I need to ask you the hugest favour *ever*. You know how much I respect you, and you know that I would help you no matter what. I have always done everything you've asked, and done you every favour you've asked for. Now, I want to ask you for a favour. It's the favour of favours. If you do this, I will do anything for you. I will be indebted to you for the rest of my life. Please, please, please! But if you can't I will understand.' Yes, I was begging.

'Out with it, Chef. I can't help you if you won't tell me what you want.'

'Mr Reinders, if you can, I will do anything. You name it: anything.'

'I can't say yes if I don't know what I'm saying yes to!'

'I beg you on my knees. Please, please can I meet Michael Jackson?'

He started laughing – I think he was waiting for me to ask the impossible.

'First tell me how many times you've dressed like him.'

'Mr Reinders, through all my teens I sang to his posters on my walls.'

'I don't mean to be difficult. But … no.'

I respected John so much that I would never argue with him or try to change his mind. I stood up and apologised for putting him in that situation. He asked me to sit back down as he required my help with another matter, but just needed Mary's go-ahead first.

'Of course, Mr Reinders. Tell me what you need – of course I will help.'

I was trying to keep my spirits up, but must have looked like a little boy whose mom had just refused to buy him the toy he wanted.

'I require catering for an event at Mahlamba Ndlopfu. I know you can't be there the whole time, but could you help me?'

'Sure, Mr Reinders. When? I will go speak to Mary.'

'I need the food there an hour before, as the president will be having a sit-down, then others will join with the media.'

'Leave it to me, Mr Reinders. Just tell me the date and time. Rest assured, it will be perfect as always.'

'Would you be there too when the food is delivered so I can run through a few things with you on the day?'

'It would be my honour, sir.' By this time, I was back in work mode, organising the event in my head.

'Thank you,' John said, and stood up. He shook my hand.

'So, Chef, can I confirm that, when the president meets Michael Jackson, you will be there with your food?'

My eyes sparkled and my blood warmed my whole body. I think I almost got an erection.

'You're joking. The event we just discussed – it's that one?'

'Mary phoned me and told me how much you harassed her, so we schemed to mess with you.'

Mary stuck her head into John's office. 'Did we get him?'

'Like you don't know. You should have seen his face!'

Once again, they had a massive laugh at my expense. I didn't care: I was going to see Michael Jackson.

I made all the food personally: every snack, every piece of bread. I even decided where each piece of garnish went. I met the King of Pop, spoke to him, and was with him before all the media and hype came in. I thought I was going to scream like a little girl, but I managed to stay composed.

If my best buddy Drugs had still been alive, I would have phoned him immediately afterwards. Lying on my bed in the hostel listening to my *Bad* CD, I would never have dreamt that, one day, I would have made food for him and met him. President Mandela, thank you – you made another dream come true.

All you need to do is Google 'celebrities visit President Mandela' to know who I have met or catered for, from soccer stars to boxing legends. It goes to show: when a duck swims on a lake, its wake starts to spread across the surface. So, too, do our wakes reach others as we swim through our lives.

It was as if President Mandela threw a bucket of water over our country, soaking us in his company and guiding us with his wisdom. As the water washed away our ignorance, it opened our eyes.

Love you always, Tata.

14
Life after Tata

When President Mandela handed over the reins of government to President Mbeki in 1999 for a well-deserved rest, I stayed on to serve the new president. I'd had dealings with President Mbeki since 1994, so we knew each other well.

I was tasked with being on the organising committee for President Mbeki's inauguration in June 1999. Using our experience from the 1994 inauguration, we organised another one to be remembered in the history books.

During the organisation period, I had to chair a meeting in the middle of the city, close to the location where the marquee was to be erected. I was running late that day, as I was receiving instructions from the Presidency about their requirements for the inauguration. I phoned ahead to apologise profusely for being late, as it was out of my control.

I arrived about twenty minutes late. As I exited the lift and walked into the foyer of the conference room, I saw a group of sub-contractors standing and waiting. As they were closest to me, I decided to start with that group and apologise to them personally and explain why I was late – to me, wasting people's time is one of the worst sins. No one person is above another.

As I walked up to the group, one of the sub-contractors asked if I was here to attend the meeting too. I said I was, and asked whether they had been informed that the meeting was running late. They said had, indeed, been informed, but that they didn't care. Before I could lay out my apology, they continued by saying that it was probably the fault of some fat-cat ANC official who did what he wanted. They went on to slander the ANC, and had a lot to say about how *they* thought things should be handled – who did the ANC think they are?

I decided that they did not deserve my apology. In fact, it annoyed me how quick people were to criticise the past five years of our country's history, with President Mandela having been nothing short of incredible.

I walked into the conference room and explained the delay to all my government colleagues. They were accommodating and understanding. I then asked whether someone could call everyone into the conference room while I unpacked my bag to get to my notes.

When everyone was seated, I introduced myself and asked each person to do the same, and to state which department or company they were from. I was chairing the meeting, so there was no time for funny drawings or people predictions. I did draw the layout of the table, though, and wrote down each person's name according to where he or she was seated.

Once everyone had introduced themselves, I asked which suppliers had been contracted to which department, and what was required of them. Once I had gathered all this information, I started with the first item on the agenda. As I was busy reading it out, I stopped. I looked up at the contractors, who were all seated in the same general area, and thought, *Screw you.*

'Please may I add an item to the agenda, one that needs to be dealt with first? Any objections?'

The attendees all shook their heads.

'Have we signed contacts with the sub-contractors, or are we still in the quotation stage?'

A lovely woman from Treasury spoke up: 'These are the contractors on the shortlist. We're awaiting final quotations.'

I looked at all my colleagues and asked whether they would have any objection to our looking for more sub-contractors.

'It won't be a problem,' one said, 'but since we have the current sub-contractors present in this meeting, are we not making them a false promise?'

I stood up and looked at them. 'I sent a message to apologise in advance for being late for this meeting, as it was not my fault. When I tried to go apologise to the sub-contractors, as I did to all of you, I had to listen to them running down our government. So, as far as I am concerned, I would rather work with people who support our government. Does anyone second my motion?'

All my colleagues put their hands up; the sub-contractors were asked to leave.

The inauguration went off perfectly. At one of the Sunday exco meetings – I was busy in the background at the meeting – President Mbeki stopped the meeting to thank me for all my efforts. His exco members even stood up and clapped. Nothing better than appreciation; there is some Madiba magic in all of us.

Speaking of exco meetings, for the first meeting that President Mbeki held I arranged the lounge as I had done for the previous five years, set up all the refreshment stations, got the lunch table ready, prepped all the food, and ensured that the meetings would continue as they always had. As the new exco members started arriving, I welcomed them and took them to the lounge. I introduced myself to the one or two whom I'd not yet met. When President Mbeki arrived, I welcomed him and escorted him up the stairs. Once I had given all the exco members their refreshments, most of the bodyguards went outside. Two remained, but out of hearing distance.

I went to the kitchen and started prepping lunch for the bodyguards. I kept an eye on the time – I normally checked on the meeting every forty-five minutes. When it was time for my first check, I took everything off the stove, removed my chef's jacket, put my suit jacket on and went into the meeting through the Pink Room so as not to disrupt the proceedings.

As I walked in and approached the attendees' chairs to fetch their empty glasses, some of the exco members stood up, upset that I was in the room and could hear what was going on. Then, I was told to get out. This confused me. I was just trying to do my job!

Flabbergasted, I started walking backwards slowly. I was just not sure what to do.

President Mbeki stood up, cleared his throat and looked at all his exco members. They stopped venting at me, but were still not amused. He started asking each one whether they knew who I was. Most of them said they knew of me, but did not know me; two of the gentlemen said that they had met me that day for the first time.

The president called me closer. I approached him reluctantly. He then asked if there had ever been a newspaper report, rumour or story that had come from the guesthouse. Everyone shook their heads. He then asked whether any of them had heard anything bad about the guesthouse in the past five years. Everyone agreed that there had been nothing negative. Then, the president informed his exco that I had been present in all meetings since the original Constitution meeting with Roelf Meyer in 1994, and that I had been present during state visit meetings involving international affairs. He then informed them all that I was welcome in all of his meetings.

That day was tense; I could feel that not everyone agreed with President Mbeki. But, as the meeting went on, I became more and more accepted – to the point of being greeted at every morning meeting with smiles and high-fives.

AFTER AN UPSETTING INCIDENT following one of our events, in which the kitchen staff and I were shouted and sworn at, I decided to resign from the guesthouse. Also, Mrs Mbeki and I did not get on; not all people do. I had served President Mbeki for a year. I had, and still have, the greatest respect for him. From what I heard in his meetings, he could have led South Africa to become one of the world's most recognised countries. He is well educated, business-savvy and worldly, and knows what our country needs. We cried when he was forced to stand down as president in 2008.

It wasn't any easy decision, but I did not want to go back to the position I'd been in when I started out at the guesthouse and struggled to be accepted. I also felt I had done my duty, and called Mary to inform her about it. She was tearful at the news and tried to convince me to stay, but in the end she accepted my resignation.

I spent some time considering my options. One night, my wife and I were invited out for dinner with friends who owned a catering company (they were a lot older than we were). After the second bottle of Boschendal Chardonnay, our friend started tearing up. My wife and I immediately worried that we'd offended this lovely lady. She explained that they had owned the catering company for over thirty years, but that things were going badly – so badly that they could lose their company.

When we got home, my wife and I agreed: we were going to assist our friends to make their company a success again.

We joined the company and, combining our new ideas with their experience, we started rebuilding. It began to grow into the giant it would become.

One afternoon in 2006, just as we were about to leave for the day, we got a call from another catering company that had tendered for a contract for a seven-day, 25 000-person function for the Independent Electoral Commission (IEC). They sought to partner with a few other catering companies that could pull it off; it was too big for them alone. I looked at my wife and the owner, and said, 'Let's go for it.'

The owner was not interested, saying that the proposal alone, let alone all the logistics, would take too many man-hours. If I compiled the whole document, I asked – the financials, logistics and tender requirements – would I be able to submit the application? He said yes, but was not eager at all.

I worked day and night to prepare the thousand-page document, and was finally ready to approach the IEC. What made the presentation even more challenging was that the event was to be hosted at the Pretoria Showgrounds. Sleep-deprived, I made an appointment to present it to the board. When I arrived, some of the board members met me in the foyer and escorted me to the conference room. I gave my whole presentation, and was told that they were impressed and interested. They were just concerned to know whether I could drive a project, as this would be one of the largest in the country.

When I stood up to explain my belief in the team and not the individual, the door opened. Everyone stood up and greeted the woman in the doorway. I knew who she was, as I had dealt with her on numerous occasions. When she greeted me as 'Chef' and knew me by name, I could see the board members looking at one another. She asked whether she could sit in on the presentation, as the onus would fall on her to sign the project off once the board members had made their choice.

They gave her the short version, explaining that they just had doubts about my capability. They felt they required a bit more due diligence on me, and some more references. Immediately, she said that she would give a reference for me, and they must know that there was no nepotism involved. We all chuckled about that one: I am white, and she is an African lady.

One board member asked, with respect, how she could give me a reference. So, she informed them that she had attended most of the functions and events I had organised and been head chef at; that I had cheffed for President Mandela's inauguration and done over forty state banquets; that I had done most of President Mandela's veterans' lunches for about 10 000 people, which she had attended; and that I had cheffed for, and been on the board of, President Mandela's inauguration. She even mentioned all the celebrities I had catered for.

She looked at me and asked why I had not submitted my CV or at least started by stating what I had done in my career. I apologised and told her that I wanted to win contracts and get work using my own abilities, not through name-dropping. She respected that; she stood up, gave me a big hug, and left. Then came all the questions from the board: they, too, were influential ANC members, and had attended events that I had done. After the meeting, I headed back to the catering company.

By the time I got there, my wife and the owner were standing outside with a bottle of champagne. My wife ran to me and jumped into my arms. 'You did it! You saved us! We got the tender!'

The owner walked up to me and hugged me. Then, he stood back: 'Well done, young man. I hope you know what you have just done.'

I was not scared. As my mate Drugs always said, 'There's the easy way, the hard way, and Brett's way.' I was going to do what I had done my whole life: jump in and make it work.

THE EVENT WAS GOING SMOOTHLY. Other departments were contacted to use our setup, procedures and logistics. Everything, but *everything*, was running without a hitch.

Until …

There was an Indian gentleman who started giving me grief about everything. He was not happy with anything, and felt that I was insensitive to his religion and culture and did not respect his beliefs. He became such a thorn in my side that he would go out of his way to moan about me to anyone who would listen. To make things worse, he was a prominent figure in the government and a senior official in the department in which he worked.

I had gone to him on numerous occasions to try to assist him and show him that I had done everything I could to accommodate him. I even showed him that the food we would serve to those with strict cultural or religious requirements would be made by sub-contractors who had the correct licences and approvals to do so.

I proved to him that I was, in fact, paying in on each meal, as I was not satisfied with the suppliers from which I had originally got quotes, and that the quality of the supplies I was using was the best in the industry. He still was not satisfied. I had 25 000 people to cook for, and one individual was causing more problems than the rest of the people involved put together.

When I could not sort this matter out by myself, I went to one of the IEC board members to raise the gentleman's concerns. I was informed that family of his had also tendered for the contract, but their company was not nearly big or experienced enough to have handled the contract. The board member also informed me that the IEC was pleased with their choice, and received nothing but compliments about my work. This was a relief; while the problems this gentleman was causing were only related to this event, he could tarnish my name for future events.

Later that afternoon, I was joking with my team. We were all tired, so I was trying to lift their spirits – most of them still work for me today, and we are like family. I am a chef who believes that, when there is a lot of pressure, time is running out and a kitchen has to produce, encouraging your team, making them laugh and encouraging them to enjoy the experience makes everything run better. It makes for the best product: all our love and enjoyment soaks into the food and the client experiences our love for what we do.

So there I was, joking and laughing. Seuntjie, one of my chefs, turned around and said, 'Hey, white man. Move away from that light. The reflection of your skin is blinding us and we are trying to work.'

All the chefs started laughing.

'Okay, all right, I will get you,' I said with a laugh, too.

Then Philip decided to jump in: 'Glad you have black buttons on your chef's jacket, otherwise we wouldn't see you standing against the white wall.'

They all started laughing even louder at me, so I joined in: 'Okay, all my chefs. When we have served dinner, you can all line up so I can give you a white eye for your comments.'

Vincent added, 'That's fine, if we can give you two black eyes – then you can be cool and wear sunglasses at night.'

'Good one,' I said. 'For that, you get two white eyes.'

We were all doing our duties and loving the atmosphere; the comments kept coming from the background.

Then: '*What?* What did you say?'

I looked at the Indian gentleman and asked him what he was doing in the kitchen – with respect, he could ask to come in; it was not protocol for him to be in the kitchen.

'Do you know who I am?'

'Yes, sir. I've been dealing with you a few times a day.'

'You are a bloody racist!'

'Sorry, sir – why would you say that?'

'I heard what you said!'

'I am sure you did. This is how we joke with each other. This is my family.'

Vincent and Philip came forward and tried to explain that we were all joking, and that there was no animosity or racism in our company. We were just messing around.

'Oh, so you are scared to tell the truth in front of the chef. You don't have to lie for him. He can't fire you. There are more of us than him – this is an ANC government.'

'Did you really just say that?' I said to him with anger – by this time, I'd had enough. 'Now you are being racist to me. Look how you are speaking to me.'

'No! I am not racist! I'm just tired of hearing the same shit all the time!'

He stormed off. I was annoyed, but my chefs told me not to take it personally. Joking, they said I should take what *they* had said to me personally instead.

We started getting very busy. It was time to load all the golf carts with food, so that it could move towards the venues. As night follows day, the gentleman came back – with police and some other government officials.

They started questioning me about what had happened. I asked them to allow me to serve the meal, and told them I would answer all their questions afterwards. The Indian gentleman was adamant that we should stop what we were doing and handle the matter immediately. I refused: if I failed to deliver one single meal, I would be in breach. Thinking about it now, I am sure this was his intention – then, his family could have taken over the contract.

While I was loading more food, the gentlemen grabbed me. I told him – in front of the police and my whole team – that, if he touched me again I would give him a hiding, not because I was racist but because I *would* hit stupid.

It was the dimmest thing I could have said. I was just so frustrated. The police officers could see that what I was doing was important and told the Indian gentleman to wait until the service was over. They would escort me and ensure I didn't disappear – as if I would run away from my team and contract.

Once all the food had gone to the venues, I went down – as I did after every meal – to check on the service and speak to different guests to ensure that they were happy with every meal they had at the function. Two police officers escorted me. I was really humiliated, but tried to ignore it so as not to make an even bigger scene.

As I was leaving the tent, Cindy, one of President Mbeki's bodyguards, came to ask me whether there was any food for them – they were the advance team for the president's function the following night, at which the election winner would be announced. I had more than enough and asked her if her team could come and grab it in the kitchen.

'Chef, why are these two police officers following you?'

I told her the story.

'*Suka, wena!*' she said to the police, telling them to leave me alone and take further instructions from her alone.

I could not stop thanking her and said that they must come for dinner – I would make it personally to thank her. While they were having their meal, the Indian gentleman came back. He wanted to handle the matter right then. Cindy stood up and chased him away. She said that President Mbeki would be at the venue the following night, and he could take up his concerns then, but until then he was not allowed to come near me. I thanked her.

'You see, Chef. White is not always right,' she said, to the laughter of the bodyguards. I joined in, too. She was just trying to do what I would do: use a joke to alleviate a bad situation.

My team and I joined the bodyguards and we all had supper. As usual, we were full of jokes and laughs.

Still, I could not sleep that night. What had happened really bugged me. How quick people are to throw the word 'racist' around, and how much it hurts, and the repercussions of doing so. Now this man wanted to take the matter to the president. Did I really need another president to vouch for me?

The next day went on as normal. We served breakfast, then lunch, and I started prepping for the formal cocktail event at which they were going to announce the winning party. I felt heavy that day; a perfectly run event can so easily be soured by something so small.

Finally, the event started. We served all the guests and, as I was walking around, running the function and serving the food, the Indian gentleman was always present; like a lion that hides in the grass, he used the crowd to conceal himself, stalking me, ready to pounce. I could see him and feel him the whole time.

After all the speeches and celebrations – the ANC had won again – the president was sitting at a cocktail table with his colleagues. I headed towards him to greet him. If the Indian gentleman made a scene, so be it. I'd done nothing wrong. The bodyguards had made a circle of protection around the president, allowing only those whom they knew had clearance to enter it. As I approached the circle, I greeted the bodyguards I hadn't seen at dinner the night before. I was a civilian now, so I no longer dealt with them all the time. Most of them were President Mandela's bodyguards who had joined President Mbeki's personal protection team.

I was a bit nervous – I no longer had clearance, and didn't know if I had the right to go wherever I pleased, like I used to. As I greeted the bodyguards and we embraced each other, they all said, 'Go see the old man. He would love to see you again.'

It felt awesome that I could still do that, and that I was still remembered.

They opened up a gap, and I walked through it to congratulate the president. As I took the first step, the gentleman made his move. The lion had his buck in a corner; it was mealtime. He stepped in behind me as if he, too, was going to the president. The next thing I heard was a thud. I looked back to see him lying on his ass, the lights on the roof as his view and his ego bleeding all over the floor. Cindy looked at me and waved me on to show that I must go ahead. With a wide, beautiful smile on her face, she winked at me. I knew what she was saying: they had my back. Just like that, the racism had become a rumour.

The president embraced me as I congratulated him and the ANC on their win. He looked at his colleagues, who knew me too, and said,

'Now we know why the food was excellent. We miss your food!'

He leant over to the table next to him and congratulated the chairperson on choosing me to do the catering. She was chuffed to get a compliment from the president.

I instructed my team to start breaking down the kitchens and infrastructure, as that was a day's work. When I went to the IEC board members to check on them again – they, too, were partying the success of the event away – they told me that, when my lion stalker had approached them, they had laughed at him. The next time he invited someone onto the dance floor, they said to him, he should first find out who he was already dancing with.

So, I grabbed a drink myself, and decided to drink all my stress away. My chefs had to drive me home that night. I woke up with a happy headache and enjoyed suffering that day while we packed up the kitchen.

Thank you, President Mandela. Even after my service to you, you were there for me.

AFTER MUCH MORE HARD WORK over the few months that followed, I decided to treat my family and go down to Cape Town. I must say, our country is magnificent.

After two weeks in Cape Town, we headed back up to Pretoria. While driving through the Free State, we decided to stop and take a break on our fifteen-hour drive. We saw a garage with a luxury resting area and nice shops up ahead, and decided that it would be a great place to stop.

While we were resting, a large convoy pulled into the same garage. I pointed it out to the boys. We spoke about the days when we were at the guesthouse. We would see these convoys all the time, but it is still a spectacular sight. We'd filled up with petrol when, behind me, I heard a familiar voice – a voice that sounded like it came from above. I swung around so fast that I was close to passing out from the g-force. There stood my president, President Mandela.

I was in shock. He wanted to know where we had just been and whether we'd enjoyed ourselves. My son was so, so happy to see his Tata. We stood speaking for a while, then his security said it was time to go. As they escorted him back to his car, I grabbed a hug and a high-five from the bodyguards. I still saw them as my friends, my long-lost friends.

As quickly as the president had appeared, he was gone.

Needless to say, everyone at the garage just stared at us. We stayed humble, and just got into the car and drove off, but what I really wanted to do was jump onto the car, doing the moonwalk and grabbing my crotch while singing 'Beat It'.

That was the last time I ever saw my president. When he died, I felt like I'd lost my grandfather. Someone I loved had died. I mourned him, and cried numerous tears for a man who had changed my life. Miss you and love you, Tata.

15
Taking flight

AFTER SEVEN YEARS, I left the catering company in 2007 and was invited to join a new wedding venue in the east of Pretoria.

I was always under the impression that it was people alone who changed me and sewed patches onto the quilt of my life. But, looking back on my years at the catering company, catering itself, for all those years, sewed a large patch onto my quilt. And it was only through the long hours at the guesthouse that I was able to handle catering.

While the guesthouse was hurry up and wait, catering was prepping all day, then packing all the trucks, then having a few hours' rest, then leaving for the function – which could take up to twenty-one hours to do. When we had our busy weekends, I would send all the trucks out then go sit in the courtyard with my phone and wait for the calls about the crises I would have to fix.

Catering made me a man in my cheffing career, if that makes any sense. At times, we would cut up tons of carcasses a day, cut up and portion tons of chicken, and load the trucks ourselves. It was incredibly physical, and the stress levels in the kitchen were far higher than they'd been at the guesthouse.

Working this hard day and night, I started losing myself. I started losing confidence – not in my career and in cheffing, but in myself. At the guesthouse, I was somebody, a piston in the engine of the kitchen machine. In catering, when I went out every weekend and cheffed for thousands, as long as the food was great and the service impeccable, no one would moan – but, when I walked around speaking to clients and trying build relationships, it was to no avail.

All the layers of confidence in myself that I had grown at the guesthouse were peeling off me, wilting where they fell.

I see this as one of the most difficult times in my marriage and home life, too. I was always tired. All I did was work. I started seeing myself as a workhorse, to be whipped and beaten when it refused to walk and turn the grindstone.

I would come home late at night, hours after my sons had fallen asleep. I would wake them up, take them to the full-length mirror in our room and take my pants off to show my sons how chafed my legs were – that, at times, they would bleed. I would show them the burn marks on my arms from the huge pots and ovens, how swollen my ankles and feet were. I wanted to show them what happens if you don't give your all at school and in the early days of your life.

My boys would grab my legs and hug me, and tell me how much they loved me, and thank me for what I was doing for them. I would beg them to listen to me: I wasn't showing them because I wanted them to know what I was doing for them. I showed them so they wouldn't end up a dumb workhorse like their dad.

I would take them to bed, kiss them goodnight and sit with them, telling them how much I loved them. Even after they'd fallen asleep, I would hold them and reassure them that I loved them with all my heart.

When I'd go back to our room, the tears would be streaming down my wife's face. They were not tears of pity or sorrow – I know, now, that it was killing her to see what had happened to me. How the work had broken me down.

My depression, and being so buggered, would make me fight with her, then go bath. Many, many a night she would wake me up in the bath and put me to bed. I still remember her running her fingers over my face, telling me that everything would be fine again and that she loved me.

I would wake up the following morning before the sun. My family would still be sleeping. After I bathed, I would take the soap and write a message on the mirror telling my wife how much I loved her, that she was my all. I'd go to the kitchen and prep my sons' breakfast, and write love messages in their fruit or use their cereal to write a message on a plate. Then off I'd go to fight another day. For the whole rotten situation to start again.

Towards the end of my time at the catering company, we were contacted by a new wedding venue to see whether we would be interested in doing its in-house catering. I saw more business, and set up the appointment. When the time came, the owner and I rushed to the venue.

When we arrived, they were in the process of installing the roof. It was the most beautiful setting; only the best was being used to build and furnish the venue. We sat at a table waiting for the owner. In walked the most beautiful lady. I swear, she was in the same class in school as Judy Michel. She was as stunning in every way, from looks to personality to composure. Even her aura was beautiful.

When she introduced herself, her name was heavenly too: 'Hi, I am Charlene.'

The builders showed us the plans and explained what they were in the process of completing. Then Charlene told us what her vision was, and what she was expecting. After the meeting, we went down to the venue to see it with our mind's eye. After the full tour, I mentioned to Charlene that the kitchen was a bit small for her vision of the kind of food and service she wanted to offer. I then went to the bar area to see what was happening. Charlene went to the builder, then to the next contractor. After her discussion with them, I went to her to beg for the opportunity to do her catering. She smiled, and told me I already had the contract – and that she believed in me, and knew I was the right person.

She then took me back to the kitchen area. She had already had the newly built walls broken down, and asked if I could stay a while longer to show the builder what I wanted for the kitchen.

We had coffee and chatted; Charlene wanted to know more about me. When the meeting was over and I'd met with the builder, I thanked her.

On the way back to the catering company, I could not stop thinking about the belief that a stranger had in me, and how she'd seen something in me that must have been so strong that she'd immediately involved me in the business. This caused more confusion than confidence. We had several more meetings with the builders and contractors, and with Charlene, to realise her vision.

Finally, it was time for the first function. It was a wedding with four hundred guests, and I was ready. It went perfectly, just as Charlene had envisaged it. When I had served all the meals, Charlene fetched me from the kitchen and started introducing me to the clients. I'd learnt they were a prominent family in the city. Charlene took me around and bragged about me to everyone; I received praise the whole evening.

That night, after packing the truck, taking my team and stock back to the catering company, and getting home, I poured a whisky and sat in the lounge in silence. I was trying to make sense of what had happened that night, and why.

My wife came in and sat next to me. She asked how the day had gone, and I told her everything. She took my arm with pride and told me that it was incredible that someone else had seen in me what she saw. I bathed and got into bed. We held each other so tight, and I slept.

The next morning, my sons woke me before my alarm did. It was still dark, so I asked if everything was okay. They jumped on me and hugged me as if my life depended on it. They were more concerned about me, as I hadn't woken them up when I'd got home the night before.

I didn't turn on the light: the tears would not stop pouring from my eyes. As I held my family, I realised, that morning, how low I had sunk.

Charlene set up a weekly meeting to discuss the functions. I started to meet her clients, design their menus and advise them about their functions. Without my knowing it, Charlene was building me up, encouraging me to become who she knew I could be. She did this naturally – and not only for me, but for everyone she interacted with. She was naturally an angel.

One day, I went to the owner of the catering company and asked him if I could be compensated for the new business I was securing. I asked him for a commission on it, as I had not had a salary increase in seven years. I showed him how the business had gone from near bankruptcy to extreme success, with trucks leaving daily for functions. He informed me that he would leave the business to me one day. Until then, I would have to work for it.

This hit me like a comet crashing down into a desert. Was this not exactly the kind of thinking that had dropped me down the well of depression? Had he not seen me as nothing more than as a workhorse to be whipped, willing to work through it in the hope of a bit of water or hay at the end of the day?

I told him that I would like to be compensated *now* for what I was doing. I could accept having done what I'd done for him for the past seven years. But now, I felt that I should earn what I deserved. All I was asking for was a small percentage on the new business that I'd bring in. He disagreed, and saw me as selfish – one day, the whole company would be mine.

I walked up to him, hugged him and, with tears in my eyes, resigned. I told him it was a pity that he couldn't see the value of what I'd done, or the extent to which I'd done it out of love for him. But if greed was his god, I didn't want to be a part of his church.

I went home and told my wife that I had resigned with a month's notice. She was ecstatic. I could see it in her eyes: first, hope that her husband was coming back to her, and then, worry about the future.

I told her I had worth and a great CV, and would find a job that suited us more. One that would make me *want* to wake up in the morning. One from which I would come home with stories about my day, not just misery and pain.

I went to see Charlene, to inform her that I had resigned and that she would be dealing with the owner from then on. I apologised for not being involved in her future. I had my contract with me, and said that she could cancel it if she wanted. As usual, we had coffee and started speaking. She wanted to know what had transpired, but only if I had already resigned. I reassured Charlene that I had. When it came to ethics and honesty, Charlene was exemplary.

I left the venue, went home and started sending my CV out. Charlene phoned, and asked if we could see her at her home that night. When my wife and I arrived, we met her husband, David. We spoke; I was offered a job. My wife was happy: I had started becoming Brett again since I'd started doing functions at Charlene's venue.

I started at the venue a month later. I missed the owner of the catering company as I still loved him. I still do – very much. Together, Charlene and I built the venue from strength to strength. Through my depression, and through all the shields I had put up, Charlene could see me for who I was.

David started getting involved. He loved the industry, the atmosphere that I had created, and the thrill of the industry's pressures. He is a highly successful man who has built up a multimillion-rand business. He is as smooth as any famous actor, and so charming. He is just as amazing as Charlene. They would take the shirts from their own backs to help people. I've always lived by Christian's saying – to be born stupid, we can handle, but to die stupid is sad – so I self-studied and am able to do electrical, plumbing, building and maintenance work myself. Then came David, a successful businessman, who could do everything I could do and more. So, I had to learn from him. He was generous and patient, and taught me everything he knew. He cooked with me during functions, and we had a blast.

In all her beauty, Charlene built me up to believe in myself in my career. I was loving it. I trained all the staff to be their best, the venue was happy and the atmosphere was one of joy. The team looked forward to coming to work, and there was always a laugh around the corner. Clients could feel what we had to offer and the business kept on growing. Charlene never stopped dreaming: soon, there were guesthouses, chapels, another venue, a restaurant. David was there the whole time – the Rock of Gibraltar, supporting and guiding and making things happen.

We were featured on several television magazine shows, and won top awards. Charlene did better than she had dreamt of doing. I was even given shares in the business as a gesture of appreciation. What beautiful people.

MY WINGS HAD MENDED. I was ready to fly.

I'd reached a stage in my life where I was ready to write a chapter of my own. I left the venue with tears and sorrow, as I would no longer be seeing Charlene and David as often. We are still friends. I will always be indebted to them; they are greater than I have described them as being.

I started looking at opening my own business, and was contracted to different companies while I did so. I ended up at a catering company that was under the umbrella of an events company. There, I met the one, the only, the great, Janine Snyders. She, too, was beautiful, funky, arty and just flipping awesome. She helped to market me in various ways, including in magazines and on radio stations.

In an interview on Jacaranda FM, I was asked where people could taste the same food that kings, queens, presidents and celebrities ate. I realised that I needed to enjoy watching my clients enjoy the food that I had cooked for royalty and heads of state, while having the opportunity to interact with them.

And so, Chefs@566 was born. It is an open kitchen where clients cook and interact with me, and I share my love of food with them. This is who, and where, I am now: loving my clients, and creating with them every day.

I was never going to write a book. At school, I could not even string five words together, let alone a whole sentence.

I took to my computer a few months ago and started typing. I didn't start with the part of my life when things were going well. I started from the beginning.

You see, I lost my father recently and had to deal with all the emotions – hate, love, forgiveness – that came with it. I got a call on a Sunday night. He said he was dying, and needed me to sort out all his financials so my mom would be fine. That is how I was told he had lung cancer.

I had to go down to his house. The discussion was hard; we were speaking as if he had already died. Then, I had to watch him die, and put his body into a body bag. I found tears, and feelings, for him that I never knew I had – that I thought he'd killed when I was a child. But, cry I did.

When the morticians had got him onto the gurney and were wheeling him down the passage, I heard my wife and mom sobbing. There was pain and hurt; my wife had known only the best of my dad.

I shouted, 'Dead man walking. No, sorry – dead man wheeling.'

The morticians were upset with me. One even swore at me: 'Sir, you are fucking sick!'

My wife jumped up, swung her arms around me and apologised

to them. She explained that this was how I dealt with pain – through my sense of humour.

My mom wanted a church service, but I refused. I had him cremated within a few days, and took his ashes to the beach. I put up his fishing rods and we had drinks for him and spread his ashes over the rocks where he'd fished for over forty years.

I knew that spot was where he found his god.

I started writing this book to heal. It came so easily: all I had to do was tell the truth.

So, yes, Dad. You hurt me, physically and emotionally. You broke me down. There were days when I was growing up that I wanted to die. When I hoped that the last punch I received when getting off the bus after school would do the trick. When I walked home depressed and sad, it was not from the beatings I took from other kids. It was from knowing I had to face you that night. Their beatings were kisses on my cheek compared to what you did.

I hated living with you. You were hard and insensitive, with a god complex. As people used to say about you: the difference between you and God was that He is really God.

Dad, I love you and forgive you. I know we both said these words. You said it with your dying breath. I really love you and forgive you.

I see, now, that you knew no better. You tried to deal with things the way you knew best. In your fucked-up way, you were trying to teach me about life and what was really going on. You didn't want me to live in a childhood cocoon. You wanted to prep me for life from day one.

Walking from Sunnyside to Brooklyn in the summer and the winter, the rain and the storms – that hour-long walk was nothing. I was so used to sitting outside schools waiting for lifts or running home from a beating or running to the village to play with my friends. You taught me that the walk was life, and had to be done.

You taught me to find recognition and love where I could, as

I was not going to get it from home. When I was approached by Christian and Judy to be trained and become someone, it was my mission to prove to you that I *would* become someone. I was looking for recognition so badly that I ran to them. I would do anything for their recognition. Their seeing me made me become a great chef. I've cheffed for more famous people than 99 per cent of all the chefs in this world.

I was not a racist and loved people of all colours. You were fair and treated everyone (everyone who did not live with us, that is) with respect, no matter their colour, religion or creed. I took beatings because I was English and you were the mine manager. That was not your fault – it was your success. And I have no right to judge you for it. Through your success, I was hated by the whiteys and made black friends. I was taught their culture and traditions.

When I joined the guesthouse and worked with different people from different cultures, I was able to relate to and understand them. I was able to be who I was without trying to fake anything, and could feel the love and respect I had from everyone. Even those who hated the whites saw me as one of their own. Thank you, Dad.

The insults that I got from the bodyguards, the kicks and the hits from the butts of their guns – they could learn from you, Dad, but I handled them. Thanks for teaching me.

I'd dealt with power in my life. I'd dealt with you every day, Dad. The difference is that all the presidents, kings, queens and celebrities saw me for who I was, Dad, and treated me with respect.

I was working for over a hundred hours a week at the catering company. I pushed through. I was not going to quit. I was not going to let you see me as a failure. You were right yet again. Thank you, Dad – you got me through long hours and physically draining times.

Dad, you did more for me than you know. You made me who and what I am today. I feel you should be proud. You did an amazing job.

I have a wife whom I've been with for longer on this earth than without. Your eldest grandchild is in his final year of Engineering studies with bursaries lined up right to his doctorate. Your other grandson is six foot five, strong as ten bears, fast as the wind, loved by all, and going to be the best chef in the world. Dad, I have the most beautiful family. We love each other, we hug each other, there is love in every second word we say to each other. I did the opposite of what you did. I could only have done that because of you. Thank you.

Dad, my wife said something the other day that really made me think. She said she was scared that if I released this book I would be criticised. What if other people did not see it the way I did? she asked. After much thought, I told her: I've been taught to handle everything life throws at me. As for people not seeing it my way, all I had to do is tell the truth. I was there, and I was blessed to have experienced it through my eyes.

I realised through all my media interviews, team building and the questions I have been asked that I should share my story. So I have, Dad. I have listened, and will be sharing my recipes and how to cook. That should make you proud, Dad. I learnt to listen.

I'm going to close my book now, and climb under my quilt, the one with all its blocks from all the wonderful people I've met and experiences I've had. I sewed those blocks onto the blanket you gave me, Dad. I am warm, safe and comfortable.

Love you, Dad. Sleep tight. I pray I see you again one day.

A selection of recipes by Christian Michel

Christian Michel

Croque-Monsieur

Fried ham and cheese Sandwiches.

3 slices of cooked ham.
12 slices of bread.
12 slices of emmental cheese.
175 gr. butter.

Preheat the oven to 220°.
Cut each slice of ham in half. On one slice of bread, place a slice of cheese, a piece of ham and another slice of cheese.
Cover with a second slice of bread. Trim the edge of the ham and cheese so they don't hang out.
Melt half of the butter in a frying pan and add the sandwiches.
Brown one side over a very moderate heat. Using a spatula and a fork, turn the sandwiches over and brown the other side, adding more butter if necessary. (This first cooking must be done slowly so that the butter does not burn and so that the cheese will stick to the bread as it begins to melt.)
Transfer the sandwiches to a baking sheet and place them in the oven.
Serve the crusty, hot sandwiches as an entré or a light lunch accompanied by a green salade.

Christian Michel

Soupe à l'oignon au fromage ou gratinée.
French onion Soup.

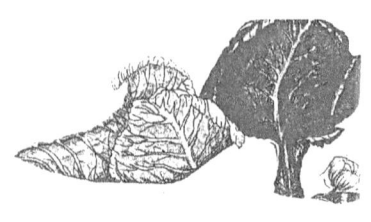

---

6 to 8 person.
900 gr. onions.
110 gr. butter.
1 clove garlic.
2 l. water.
86 gr. gruyère cheese.
40 gr. flour.

Slice onion thinly, slowly fry a light gold in the butter with the crushed garlic, dust with flour.
Fry flour golden and add water.
Add salt and pepper and simmer until onions are tender, remove fat.
Place small slice of bread and the cheese cut in thin small slice in a soup tureen or individual soup bowls.
Pour the boiling hot soup on top, cover, and allow to stand 5-6 minutes before serving.
This soup can also be served au "GRATIN" in fireproof bowls, in this case use less water so that the soup is a little thicker.

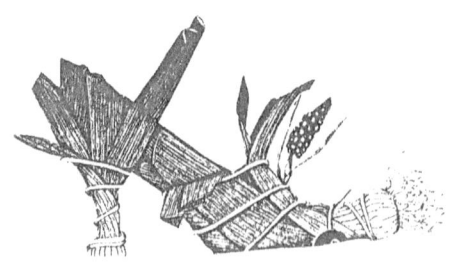
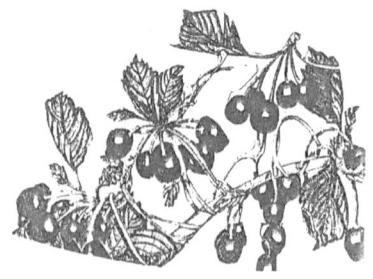

Christian Michel

gratin Dauphinois

6 persons.
1 kg. potatoes.
1 egg.
30 gr. butter.
280 ml. milk.
80-100 gr. gruyère or emmentaler cheese.
garlic.
nutmeg.   Cooking time 40-45 minutes.

Rub a baking dish generously with garlic, butter it thickly and fill with raw, peeled potatoes cut in thin slices, seasoned with salt, pepper and nutmeg.

Beat the egg, mix with cold milk, pour over potatoes so that they are fully covered and baked in a moderate oven.

Cut cheese in small thin slices and mix with potatoes. It can, however, be omitted.

This potatoes dish can be cooked two or three days in advance. If so, you can add a little milk before warming up.

Christian Michel

Truites aux amandes.

Trout with almonds.

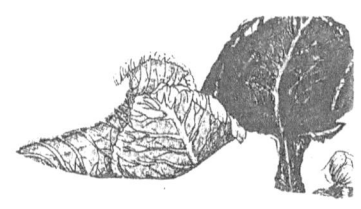

---

4 persons.
4 trouts.
salt. pepper.
50 gr. flour.
75 gr. butter.
100 gr. flaked almonds.

Gut the trout but leave their heads on. Wash them, dry carefully on absorbent paper, season and toss lightly in flour.
Heat 50 gr. butter in a frying pan or oil.
Place the trout in it.
Brown them well over a moderate heat.
Arrange the trout on a heated serving dish and keep hot.
Put the butter to the frying pan and use to sauté the flaked almonds. Cook until golden brown then sprinkle over the trouts. Pour the juices from the pan over all. Garnish each trout with two lemons slices and sprinkle one of these with chopped parsley.
Serve very hot.

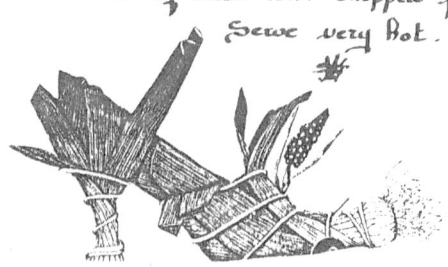

Christian Michel
Crème Caramel

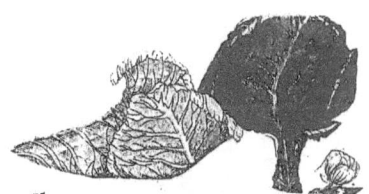

For 10 persons	For 15 persons
250 gr. sugar	375 gr. sugar
1 liter milk	1½ liter milk
8 egg yolks	12 egg yolks
4 eggs	6 eggs
Vanilla essence	Vanilla essence

Put the eggs and egg yolks into mixing bowls with sugar and mix until cream.
Heat the milk with vanilla essence. Let it cool.
Mix all ingredients slowly and let the mixture rest over night.

Pour caramelized sugar into a plain dry mould.
The caramelized sugar must be cold.

Pour the custard mixture into the mould with the caramelized sugar and place the mould in a pan with water and bake in the oven for ± 45 minutes at 150°.

Serve chilled, or room temperature.
This crème caramel can be prepared two or three days in advance.

Acknowledgements

AGAIN, TO MY ALL, TRACEY LADDS – I apologise for being me.

To Keagan Ladds, my miracle child. Max Ladds, from my shadows, you will rise to become the giant you deserve to become. Charles Ladds – you see, Dad, beatings do pay off.

To Christian and Judy Michel – love you, love you, love you. Joe and Hildegard Schanding, Africa hasn't been the same since you arrived. Thank you for your love. Charlene and David Georgiades – keep changing lives, power people.

Christiaan, my Stoffie van den Berg, after all these years of working together, hell has no idea what is coming. Philip Human – no white eye, but I still love you after working with you for nineteen years. Janine Snyders, your belief in me started me on this path. Tamaryn Leigh, with your support I will always be great. Mathew Mathews, belief in me from a man of your stature is worth more than all the water in the sea. Pieter van Heerden, my awesome friend, now and forever.

Annie Olivier, if people could just be blessed to meet you, they would know how great you are. Thank you: this is all thanks to you. Angela Voges, I thank you for being so amazing, and for understanding Chef.

And to my president, Tata Mandela. You showed me life when I did not believe I needed direction. You loved me when I did not realise I needed love. You made my future while I was serving you. May all those who knew you spread the word about how truly awesome you were.

Sitting at President Mandela's desk.

BRETT LADDS *served as the executive chef of the South African government from 1994 to 2000 under presidents Nelson Mandela and Thabo Mbeki. During this time he managed the Presidential Guesthouse, cooked daily for the president and his guests and catered for 54 state banquets.*

Today he owns Chefs@566 restaurant in Pretoria and is also involved in the Mercedes-Benz Lifestyle Avantgarde Bistro. Ladds has been a partner in a number of catering companies and has catered for up to 25 000 people. He has also worked at Avianto in Muldersdrift, Johannesburg.

Ladds studied at Fleur de Lys in Pretoria and trained under Chef Christian Michel from 1992 until 1994. Michel was the executive chef of the South African government from the 1960s until his retirement in 1991.

www.ingramcontent.com/pod-product-compliance
Lightning Source LLC
Chambersburg PA
CBHW060834190426

43197CB00039B/2586